HAVING AUTHORITY
The Origins and Development of Priesthood During the Ministry of Joseph Smith

HAVING AUTHORITY
The Origins and Development of Priesthood During the Ministry of Joseph Smith

By Gregory A. Prince

John Whitmer
Historical Association
Monograph Series

Independence Press
Independence, Missouri

Prince, Gregory A., 1950–
   Having Authority : The Origins and Development of
Priesthood during the Ministry of Joseph Smith / by
Gregory A. Prince.
      p.   cm.—(John Whitmer Historical Association
monograph series)
   Includes bibliographical references and index.
   ISBN 0-8309-0635-5
   1. Smith, Joseph, 1805–1844—Contributions to Mor-
mon doctrine of priesthood. 2. Aaronic priesthood
(Mormon Church)—History of doctrines—19th century.
3. Melchizedek priesthood (Mormon Church)—History
of doctrines—19th century. 4. Authority (Religion)—
History of doctrines—19th century. 5. Mormon
Church—Doctrines—History—19th century. 6. Mormon Church—Government—History—19th century. I.
Title. II. Series: Monograph series (John Whitmer Historical Association)
BX8659.P75   1993
262'.1493—dc20   93-10136
                                                      CIP

97 96 95 94 93   1 2 3 4 5

Dedication

This monograph is dedicated to the memory of Jack W. Carlson, who died tragically and suddenly in December 1992. His close friendship and constant encouragement over the past decade were essential to the completion of this project. I shall miss him greatly.

Table of Contents

Foreword

This publication is the second contribution to the series of monographs in Restoration history published for the John Whitmer Historical Association by Independence Press. The idea for this series arose when Roger Yarrington, editorial director for the press, proposed publishing at no expense to the association a series of historical monographs on Mormon history produced under the editorial direction of JWHA. It was a forward-looking prospect, as association members had been trying for some time to find an appropriate outlet for historical scholarship that was not long enough for a book but could not be condensed to the length of an article.

In 1992 the first monograph in the series appeared, *Hero or Traitor*, Marjorie Newton's biographical study of Charles W. Wandell, the man most responsible for the founding of both the Utah-based Latter-day Saint and the Midwest-based Reorganized Church missions in Australia. This work has enjoyed a warm response from the scholarly community.

The second volume in the series deals with the important and little-understood development of the priesthood structure in the early Latter Day Saint tradition. Gregory A. Prince, a scientist and medical practitioner in the Washington, D.C., area, has spent years researching the evolution of the Mormon priesthood. His insights into the development of this hierarchy offer a useful corrective and a much-needed expansion on previous conceptions of priesthood authority, organization, and function. He finds the story neither so simplistic nor "cut and dried" as has been taught in most church school classes. Instead, there was a sophisticated synergy between local expediency, historical trends, and theological determinants in the definition of priesthood.

The John Whitmer Historical Association invites other authors who have monograph-length studies to submit them for consideration. Please send them to the John Whitmer Historical Association Monograph Editor, Graceland College, Lamoni, IA 50140.

Roger Launius

Preface

In 1977 W. Don Ladd, president of the Washington, D.C., Stake of the Church of Jesus Christ of Latter-day Saints, called me to be president of the Elders Quorum of the Gaithersburg Ward. Neither he nor I appreciated ·at the time the consequences of his action. In attempting to understand the calling—and priesthood in general—I was frustrated by the lack of published material on the subject. John A. Widtsoe's *Priesthood and Church Government,* which had been a priesthood course of study and was considered the standard LDS reference on the subject, had been written four decades earlier and was essentially a scrapbook of quotations with minimal historical and analytical content. No other comprehensive book on the subject had been written in the LDS Church since Widtsoe's.

I served as Elders Quorum president until 1981 but continued thereafter to be fascinated by the subject of priesthood and frustrated by the paucity of published material. In 1985 I decided to attempt a comprehensive study of priesthood and began to gather primary source material, entering it into a computerized database. That database, which spans the entire history of the Latter-day Saint movement, now exceeds 10,000 pages.

This monograph will be part of a book on priesthood during the lifetime of Joseph Smith. In writing it I have been heavily dependent on the support of my wife, JaLynn, who sensed earlier than I the importance of this project. In addition to the resources of my own library, I have drawn on archival material from the Archives of the Church of Jesus Christ of Latter-day Saints in Salt

Lake City, Utah; the Library-Archives of the Reorganized Church of Jesus Christ of Latter Day Saints in Independence, Missouri; The Huntington Library in San Marino, California; and the Harold B. Lee Library at Brigham Young University in Provo, Utah. I am grateful to the staff of each of these institutions and for the permission each has given for the use of the materials cited in this monograph.

Although I had originally envisioned writing an entire book before publishing anything, Roger Launius, currently president of the John Whitmer Historical Association, suggested that I consider the JWHA Monograph Series for the material on priesthood rstoration. He and Richard Brown, of Herald Publishing House which publishes the JWHA series through Independence Press, have been most helpful in bringing the manuscript to published form. I am grateful also to Lester Bush and Val Hemming for critical review of the manuscript.

At the 1991 annual meeting of the Mormon History Association, Paul Edwards kindly suggested that I quit goofing off and start writing. The following year an abbreviated version of this monograph was presented at the MHA meeting in St. George, Utah. To get even, I suggested to the program chairman that Paul be considered to respond to the paper. As usual, he took the task seriously. His critique is published as part of this monograph with his permission.

Gregory A. Prince

HAVING AUTHORITY
The Origins and Development of Priesthood During the Ministry of Joseph Smith

By Gregory A. Prince

The Latter Day Saint tradition declares itself unique, basing its claim largely on the belief that Joseph Smith was the recipient of divinely bestowed authority. The accounts of the restoration of authority describe events within space and time, mentioning places, dates, names, and circumstances; thus, they are susceptible to critical analysis. Yet, despite the central importance of authority within the tradition, no adequate description of its development exists.

Although the term "priesthood" is now synonymous with authority, this relationship—and even the concept of priesthood as now understood—did not develop until several years after the beginning of the Restoration.[1] Initially authority was understood to be inherent in

---

1. "Restoration" will be used throughout this monograph to apply generally to the Latter Day Saint tradition during the ministry of Joseph Smith. The Church of Jesus Christ of Latter-day Saints, with headquarters in Salt Lake City, Utah, will be

what are now termed "offices." The terms and concepts of "Aaronic Priesthood" and "Melchizedek Priesthood," universally used by the LDS and RLDS churches today, were not adopted until 1835 and underwent significant changes as late as 1844, the year of Joseph Smith's death. Three offices—elder, priest, and teacher—were present within the Restoration by August 1829, as were the ordinances of baptism, confirmation, and ordination, but the word "priesthood" in reference to these offices and ordinances did not occur for another three years.[2] Finally, while important steps in this developmental process were early associated with divine or angelic visitations, specific roles for John the Baptist and Peter, James, and John were first identified only several years later. Though today still associated with the restoration of Aaronic and Melchizedek priesthoods, during Joseph Smith's lifetime they became completely overshadowed by the Old Testament prophet Elijah. Indeed, after 1840 Smith never associated John the Baptist or Peter, James, and John with the concept of priesthood, opting instead to emphasize the primacy of Elijah.[3]

---

abbreviated "LDS," and the Reorganized Church of Jesus Christ of Latter Day Saints, with headquarters in Independence, Missouri, will be abbreviated "RLDS." Also, the LDS spelling of "Melchizedek" will be used throughout rather than the RLDS "Melchisedec."

2. This monograph is part of a larger study that will also include discussions of the offices and ordinances which became associated with structured authority.

3. Inasmuch as this analysis of Restoration authority will draw conclusions which differ from the current understanding of many Latter Day Saints, it will be important for the reader to set

Thus, the claim of divinely restored authority was present before the organization of the church, but the structure and nomenclature of authority developed markedly throughout the remaining years of Joseph Smith's life. Although the development occurred along a continuum, the continuity was punctuated by several key events. In attempting to understand the developmental process, it is useful to divide the continuum into several phases on the basis of those events.

---

aside, momentarily, his or her preconceptions. This monograph was developed using "historical-critical" methodology. Originally developed as a tool for studying the Bible, "it is a method for *collecting* all possible witnesses to an era or event, *evaluating* what they say, *relating* the findings to one another in a coherent structure, and *presenting* the conclusions with the evidence" (Krentz and Edgar, *The Historical-Critical Method* [Philadelphia: Fortress Press, 1975], 41 [emphasis in the original]). Ideally, this approach minimizes the effect of the historian's own bias, as he or she allows the historical record to speak in as clear a voice as possible. However, at the same time that the historian must allow each source to "speak in its own voice," his or her role must not be passive. The responsibility is to determine not merely what happened but what the significance of past happenings was and is. Much as the scientist, the historian must collect data, determine their credibility, draw conclusions from their analysis, and then (most importantly) formulate new hypotheses to fuel the engine of further inquiry. Regardless of the authorship of sources consulted for this paper, each record has been allowed to speak for itself. While there are no set rules for determining authenticity of a source, I have applied two general criteria to all sources. First, an account written by a participant in an event is more likely to accurately portray the event than one written by a nonparticipant. Second, the briefer the interval between the event and the writing of the record describing it, the more likely the record will accurately portray the event.

Phase I: September 1823 to March 1829— "Implicit Authority"

Joseph Smith held a unique position within the Restoration from its beginning, due to his relationship with Moroni, the guardian of the "gold plates" of the Book of Mormon, a relationship that began in 1823. His authority to act in God's name, however, was implicit rather than explicit. His primary concerns during this time were his own status with God and the obtaining and translating of the plates. Because he expressed no intention of organizing a church, nor of conferring authority or ordinances on others, explicit authority seems not to have been an issue, as shown by the three known revelations dating from this period. In the first, from July 1828, he was chastised for having lost part of the Book of Mormon manuscript and was told that he would again be called to the work of translation, but no formal authority was described.[4] In the second, dated February 1829, a ministry extending beyond the translation and publication of the Book of Mormon was inferred, and the qualifications for that ministry were listed: "Faith, hope, charity and love, with an eye single to the glory of God."[5] Explicit authority, conferred either through divine or human ordination, was not mandated. The third revelation, given to Joseph Smith one month later in behalf of Martin Harris, described for the first time the establishment of a church, "like unto the church which was taught by my disciples in the days

---

4. *A Book of Commandments, for the Government of the Church of Christ, Organized According to Law, on the 6th of April, 1830* (Independence, Missouri: W. W. Phelps & Co., 1833), II:1-6. Hereafter, references to this book will be abbreviated *BC*.

5. *BC* III:1.

of old,"[6] but stated no requirement for explicit authority.[7]

Phase II: April 1829 to October 1830— "Angelic Authority"

In April 1829, Oliver Cowdery arrived in Harmony, Pennsylvania, to be Smith's new scribe. Within days, their work on the Book of Mormon involved passages dealing with baptism. The first of these was from the Book of Mosiah:[8]

And now it came to pass that Alma took Helam, he being one of the first, and went and stood forth in the water,

---

6. *BC* IV:5.
7. When this revelation was revised before its 1835 publication in *Doctrine and Covenants of The Church of the Latter Day Saints: Carefully Selected from the Revelations of God* (Kirtland, Ohio: F. G. Williams & Co., 1835; hereafter abbreviated *DC, 1835*), three new passages were added reflecting a subsequent consciousness of a need for formal authority: "...hereafter you shall be ordained and go forth and deliver my words unto the children of men" (*DC, 1835* XXXII:2); "...whom I shall call and ordain...you must wait yet a little while; for ye are not yet ordained" (Ibid., verse 3).
8. Although references to baptism occur in "The First Book of Nephi" and "The Second Book of Nephi," which precede "The Book of Mosiah," the work of translation, which had been suspended by the loss of 116 pages of manuscript by Martin Harris, resumed with the translation of "The Book of Mosiah," proceeded through "The Book of Moroni," then commenced anew with "The First Book of Nephi." Therefore, the references to baptism in "The First Book of Nephi" and "The Second Book of Nephi" were translated *after* those in "The Book of Mosiah." Oliver Cowdery also mentioned references to the risen Christ's ministry to the Americas, in "The Book of Nephi, the Son of Nephi, Which was the Son of Helaman," as motivating Smith and himself to seek authority to baptize (*Latter Day Saints' Messenger and Advocate* 1, no. 1 [Kirtland, Ohio: October 1834]: 15-16).

and cried, saying, O Lord, pour out thy spirit upon thy servant, that he may do this work with holiness of heart. And when he had said these words, the spirit of the Lord was upon him, and he said, Helam, I baptize thee, having authority from the Almighty God, as a testimony that ye have entered into a covenant to serve him until you are dead, as to the mortal body; and may the spirit of the Lord be poured out upon you; and may he grant unto you eternal life, through the redemption of Christ, which he hath prepared from the foundation of the world. And after Alma had said these words, both Alma and Helam was [sic] buried in the water; and they arose and came forth out of the water rejoicing, being filled with the spirit. And again, Alma took another, and went forth a second time into the water, and baptized him according to the first, only he did not bury himself again in the water.[9]

Four parts of this passage are of particular importance. First, before Alma could baptize anyone, it was necessary that he receive authority directly from God. Second, authorization came in the form of "the spirit of the Lord" being upon him, with no mention either of angelic appearance or of the laying on of hands. Third, Alma baptized himself and Helam simultaneously. Finally, although Alma acted under divine authorization, no ordained office was mentioned.

Moved by the Book of Mormon passages, Smith and Cowdery went to the waters of the Susquehanna River in anticipation of baptism and there were given author-

---

9. *The Book of Mormon: An Account Written by the Hand of Mormon, Upon Plates Taken from the Plates of Nephi* (Palmyra, New York: E. B. Grandin, 1830; hereafter abbreviated *BM, 1830*), "The Book of Mosiah," chapter IX, page 192. Compare the current LDS edition of the Book of Mormon (Mosiah 18:12-13) and the RLDS editions (Mosiah 9:43-46).

ity to baptize each other. Although the Book of Mormon references to Alma's baptism may have motivated them to seek this ordinance, only in two respects (divine authorization and the absence of reference to a specific office) did their experience parallel that of Alma, as shown in the earliest known description of their baptism:

Now therefore whosoever repenteth & humbleth himself before me & desireth to be baptized in my name shall ye baptize them. And after this manner did he [the Lord] command me that I should baptize them Behold ye shall go down & stand in the water & in my name shall ye baptize them. And now behold these are the words which ye shall say calling them by name saying Having authority given me of Jesus Christ I baptize you in the name of the Father & of the Son & of the Holy Ghost Amen. And then shall ye immerse them in the water & come forth again out of the water & after this manner shall ye baptize in my name.[10]

Later accounts highlighted the two respects in which their experience differed from that of Alma: (1) they received authority under the hands of an angel; and (2) they baptized each other, rather than either one baptizing himself as Alma had done.

Although they now possessed authority to baptize, they did not have the higher authority mentioned in

---

10. "The Articles of the Church of Christ," written by Oliver Cowdery in 1829. The original is in the Archives Division, Church Historical Department, The Church of Jesus Christ of Latter-day Saints, Salt Lake City, Utah (hereafter abbreviated "LDS Archives"); the document has been published in Robert J. Woodford, "The Historical Development of the Doctrine and Covenants" (Ph.D. Dissertation, Brigham Young University, 1974), 288. This dissertation is available from University Microfilms International (Ann Arbor, Michigan), order #8027231.

later dictated passages of the Book of Mormon, which enabled the recipients to confer the Holy Ghost and to ordain priests and teachers. In the later passages, those holding this higher authority were called by two names, "Disciple" and "Elder," and had authority equivalent to that given by Christ to his apostles in Palestine.[11] David Whitmer later said that Smith and Cowdery obtained this authority early in June 1829 after he took them to his father's farm in Fayette, New York, and that following this they ordained each other elders.[12] Shortly thereafter, Whitmer was baptized and ordained the third elder of the Restoration.[13]

Inasmuch as a revelation dated mid-June stated that Cowdery and Whitmer already had been "called even with that same calling" as the Apostle Paul,[14] it is clear that the restoration of higher authority occurred within the first two weeks of June 1829. This same revelation reinforced the idea that the higher authority was the same described in the Book of Mormon, as it stated of the twelve disciples Cowdery and Whitmer were to choose, "You are they which are ordained of me to ordain priests and teachers," the same duty given the

11. *BM, 1830,* "The Book of Moroni," chapters II and III, pp. 574-575.
12. "Questions asked of David Whitmer at his home in Richmond Ray County Mo. Jan 14—1885, relating to Book of Mormon, and the history of the Church of Jesus Christ of LDS by Elder Z. H. Gurley," Ms d 4681, LDS Archives; original in Library-Archives, Reorganized Church of Jesus Christ of Latter Day Saints, Independence, Missouri (hereafter abbreviated as RLDS Library-Archives).
13. David Whitmer, *An Address to All Believers in Christ* (Richmond, Missouri: 1887), 32.
14. *BC* XV:11. For the dating of this revelation, see Woodford, 263-267.

twelve disciple/elders in the Book of Moroni.[15]

Both Mormon and non-Mormon records pre-dating 1836 support the claim of divine or angelic restoration of authority, although the angels were not named until 1835:

- 1829: Oliver Cowdery wrote that the authority "given me of Jesus Christ" was essential to performing baptisms.[16] Later accounts which spoke of the voice of Jesus in association with the visit of the angel were consistent with this earliest account.

- 1 June 1830: The non-Mormon *Palmyra Reflector* referred to Oliver Cowdery as an "apostle...under a command."[17]

- 16 November 1830: The non-Mormon *Painesville Telegraph*, referring to Oliver Cowdery, said he "pretends to have a divine mission, and to have seen and conversed with Angels."[18]

- 7 December 1830: The same newspaper reported claims that "Mr. Oliver Cowdry has his commission directly from the God of Heaven, and that he has his credentials, written and signed by the hand of Jesus Christ, with whom he has personally conversed, and as such, said Cowdry claims that he and his associates are the only persons on earth who are qualified to administer in his name. By this authority, they proclaim to the world, that all who do not believe *their* testimony, and be baptised by them for the remission of their sins...must be forever miserable."[19]

---

15. *BC* XV: 35. Compare *BM, 1830*, "The Book of Moroni," chapter III, page 575.
16. "The Articles of the Church of Christ," in Woodford, 288.
17. *Palmyra (New York) Reflector* (1 June 1830).
18. *Painesville (Ohio) Telegraph* (16 November 1830).
19. Ibid. (7 December 1830).

- 14 February 1831: The *Palmyra Reflector* published an account of the preaching of the Mormon missionaries, saying that "they then proclaimed that there had been no religion in the world for 1500 years,— that no one had been authorized to preach and teach for that period,—that Joseph Smith had now received a commission from God for that purpose.... Smith (they affirmed) had seen God frequently and personally—Cowdery and his friends had frequent interviews with angels...."[20]

- 19 April 1831: The *Painesville Telegraph* published a letter from Martin Harris which included the earliest published version of "The Articles and Covenants of the Church of Christ." Greatly expanded compared to its 1829 predecessor, it stated that Smith and Cowdery were each "called of God and ordained an apostle of Jesus Christ, an elder of the church."[21]

- Late 1832: Joseph Smith, when he began to write his autobiography between July and November 1832,[22] opened the account by reciting, chronologically, the early events of the Restoration, the third of which was "the reception of the holy Priesthood by the minist[e]ring of Aangels to admin[i]ster the letter of the Gospel the Law and commandments as they were given unto him and the ordinenc[e]s."[23]

- 2 March 1833: A Protestant minister in Ohio, in a letter to another minister, wrote: "The following Curious occurrence occurred last week in Newburg

---

20. *Palmyra Reflector* (14 February 1831).
21. *Painesville Telegraph* (19 April 1831).
22. See Dean C. Jessee, *The Personal Writings of Joseph Smith* (Salt Lake City, Utah: Deseret Books, 1984), 640, note 6.
23. Ibid., 4.

about 6 miles from this Place [Cleveland]. Joe Smith the great Mormonosity was there and held forth, and among other things he told them he had seen Jesus Christ and the Apostles and conversed with them, and that he could perform Miracles."[24]

- 18 December 1833: A blessing given by Joseph Smith to Oliver Cowdery spoke of the fulfillment in Oliver "of a prophecy of Joseph, in ancient days, which he said should come upon the Seer of the last days and the Scribe that should sit with him, and that should be ordained with him, by the hand of the angel in the bush, unto the lesser priesthood, and after receive the holy priesthood under the hands of those who had been held in reserve for a long season even those who received it under the hand of the Messiah."[25]

- 12 February 1834: In a meeting preparatory to the organization of the first high council, Joseph Smith said: "I shall now endeavour to set forth before this council, the dignity of the office which has been

---

24. Reverend Richmond Taggart to Reverend Jonathon Goings (2 March 1833); original in the American Baptist Historical Society, Rochester, New York.

25. Blessing given 18 December 1833 by Joseph Smith, Jr., to Oliver Cowdery; original in Patriarchal Blessing Book 1, LDS Archives; photocopy of the original in the author's possession. Although this blessing was given in 1833, it was not recorded in the Patriarchal Blessing Book until 2 October 1835. While it could be claimed that Cowdery "updated" the content of the blessing when he entered it in the book, two factors argue in favor of its integrity having been preserved. First, the angels were not named, even though revised revelations in the Doctrine and Covenants, published earlier in 1835, had named them. Second, the same book used the terms "Aaronic Priesthood" and "Melchizedek Priesthood," yet the 1833 blessing retained the earlier terms, "lesser priesthood" and "holy priesthood," rather than borrowing, anachronistically, the later ones.

conferred upon me by the ministering of the Angel of God, by his own voice and by the voice of this Church."[26]

- October 1834: In a letter published in the church newspaper, Oliver Cowdery described the restoration of authority to baptize. This was the first time a published Mormon source specifically linked the visit of an angel with the restoration of this authority (although the angel was not named): "'Twas the voice of the angel from glory...we received under his hand the holy priesthood, as he said, 'upon you my fellow servants, in the name of Messiah I confer this priesthood and this authority....'"[27]

- 21 February 1835: In instructing the newly chosen Quorum of Twelve Apostles, Oliver Cowdery said: "You have been ordained to the Holy Priesthood. You have received it from those who had their power and Authority from an Angel."[28]

- Mid-1835: With the publication of the Doctrine and Covenants, several previously published revelations were revised, among which was one dated September 1830. Whereas the earlier version had made no mention of angelic visitations, this version now recounted the restoration of both levels of authority, identifying for the first time the restorers as "John the son of Zacharias, which Zacharias he (Elias) visited and gave promise that he should have a son, and his name should be John, and he should be filled with the spirit

26. "Kirtland High Council Minutes" (12 February 1834), LDS Archives.
27. *Latter Day Saints' Messenger and Advocate* 1, no. 1 (Kirtland, Ohio: October 1834): 15-16.
28. "Kirtland High Council Minutes" (21 February 1835).

of Elias; which John I have sent unto you, my servants, Joseph Smith, jr. and Oliver Cowdery, to ordain you unto this first priesthood which you have received, that you might be called and ordained even as Aaron.... And also with Peter, and James, and John, whom I have sent unto you, by whom I have ordained you and confirmed you to be apostles and especial witnesses of my name, and bear the keys of your ministry...."[29]

---

29. *DC, 1835* L:2, 3. While it is not known why Smith and Cowdery delayed naming the messengers until 1835, six years after the fact, it is possible that they gave early priority to the Book of Mormon and its messenger, Moroni, since the book had served as the model for the early church and both levels of authority derived from it. Thus, in the earliest years, it would have been logical for them to give priority to Moroni, rather than to other messengers then viewed as subordinate to him. Not until later would they begin to attribute greater importance to the events of 1829, with the increasing importance reflected in the greater detail of later accounts. In a similar fashion, as will be shown later in this monograph, the linkage between Elijah and priesthood was not made until 1838, whereupon Elijah's role quickly overshadowed those of John the Baptist and Peter, James, and John. Although the association of angels with the restoration of authority was made at an early date, two important figures within the early years of the Restoration, David Whitmer and William McLellin, later denied that association. Because of their prominence, it is important to examine their claims.

In 1885, Zenas Gurley, Jr., a prominent elder in the RLDS Church, interviewed David Whitmer and asked about the restoration of authority to baptize:

Q: Can you tell why that Joseph and Oliver were ordained to the lesser Priesthood by the hand of an Angel but in receiving the Higher they ordained each other?

A: I moved Joseph Smith and Oliver Cowdery to my fathers house in Fayette Seneca County New York, from Harmony, Penn. in the year 1829, on our way I conversed freely with them upon this great work they were bringing about, and Oliver stated to me in Josephs presence that they had

baptized each other seeking by that to fulfill the command....
I never heard that an Angel had ordained Joseph and Oliver
to the Aaronic priesthood until the year 1834 5 or 6—in Ohio.
My information from Joseph and Oliver upon this matter
being as I have stated, and that they were commended so to
do by revealment through Joseph. I do not believe that John
the Baptist ever ordained Joseph and Oliver as stated and
believed by some. I regard that as an error, a misconception.
—Gurley interview; see footnote 12.

William McLellin, a charter member of the Quorum of Twelve
Apostles organized in 1835, was not associated with the Restoration until 1831, two years after the restoration of lesser and
higher authority. Many years later, he vehemently denied angelic
intervention:

"...as to the story of John, the Baptist ordaining Joseph and
Oliver on the day they were baptized: I never heard of it in
the church for years, altho I carefully noticed things that were
said. And today I do not believe the story" (William E. McLellin
to Joseph Smith III, July 1872; RLDS Library-Archives,
Miscellaneous Letters and Papers, P13, f213).

Similarly, neither man endorsed the concept of an angelic
restoration of the higher authority.

While it is possible that neither Whitmer nor McLellin had
heard of angelic restoration of authority before the publication
of the 1835 Doctrine and Covenants, it is clear that many other
people, both within and without the church, were familiar with
the story. The refusal of either man to acknowledge the story
may have been due to the time between its occurrence (1829)
and their accounts (forty-three years for McLellin, fifty-six years
for Whitmer); a belief that all necessary authority came through
the events surrounding the Book of Mormon or, in the case of
Whitmer, a consistent refusal to acknowledge as valid any
visitations or visions in which he, himself, had not been a
participant. Thus, he vigorously defended the Book of Mormon
and his own vision of Moroni, yet he declined to validate such
crucial Restoration events as Joseph Smith's "First Vision," the
restoration events of 1829, the vision of the "degrees of glory" in
1832, the vision of the Celestial Kingdom in 1836, or the 1836
appearances of Jesus Christ, Moses, Elias, and Elijah in the
newly dedicated Kirtland "House of the Lord"—in none of which
had he been a participant. (The vision of the "degrees of glory"
is contained in *DC, 1835* XCI; the vision of the Celestial Kingdom
in the current LDS edition of the Doctrine and Covenants
[hereafter abbreviated *DC, LDS*] Section 137; and the appearances of Jesus Christ, Moses, Elias, and Elijah in *DC, LDS* 110.)

It is important at this point to summarize the status of "authority" in 1829. Because of passages in the Book of Mormon, Smith and Cowdery sought authority to baptize, which they received through angelic intervention. Additional passages in the book described a higher authority (to confer the Holy Ghost and to ordain to offices) which they subsequently received, again through angelic intervention. At that time, neither level of authority was called "priesthood." Indeed, before 1831 the only use of the term "priesthood" within the Restoration was in the Book of Mormon, where it was used synonymously with the office of high priest,[30] an office which did not exist within the Restoration until late 1831. Before 1831, men acted by virtue of the authority inherent in the office to which they had been ordained, either elder, priest, or teacher. In performing ordinances, they sometimes referred to their authority explicitly, as in the baptismal prayer which began, "Having authority given me of Jesus Christ...."[31] Even when explicit, however, the reference to authority did not use the term "priesthood." More often, authority was implied, as in the blessing of the bread and wine,[32] and in the ordination of priests and teachers.[33] As will be shown later in this monograph, it was several

---

30. *BM, 1830*, "The Book of Alma, the Son of Alma," chapters IX and X, pp. 258-260.
31. "The Articles of the Church of Christ," in Woodford, 288.
32. *BM, 1830*, "The Book of Moroni," chapters IV and V, pp. 575-576.
33. Ibid., chapter III, page 575. Within the LDS Church, the prayers currently used for the Sacrament of the Lord's Supper and for baptism are essentially the same as those used in 1829 and 1830, and still do not employ the term "priesthood." By contrast, use of the prescribed ordination prayer for LDS priests and teachers (in the Book of Mormon) was discontinued, and current

months after the June 1831 General Conference at which the "high priesthood" was conferred that the term "priesthood" began to enter common usage.

Although the Book of Mormon named priest and teacher as the two offices possessing the lesser authority, neither Joseph Smith nor Oliver Cowdery stated that they had been ordained to either of the two offices but simply that they had received authority from the angel.[34] Indeed, the Book of Mormon stated that both offices had authority to baptize.[35] It was not until 1831 that a revised version of the "Articles and Covenants" of the church detailed the duties of priests and teachers, restricting the performing of baptisms to the former office.[36]

The higher authority, according to the Book of Mormon, resided in men who were called both disciples and elders, and whose authority was equal to that of the Jerusalem apostles.[37] Initially, the Restoration applied

---

instructions mandate that prayers used in all ordinations, as well as all other ordinances except baptism and the Sacrament of the Lord's Supper, state that the officiator acts by authority of the "priesthood." See *General Handbook of Instructions* (Corporation of the President of The Church of Jesus Christ of Latter-day Saints, 1989), Section 5, pages 1-5.

34. Even Smith's most detailed account, published in 1842, which applied the term "priesthood" retroactively, stated that (1) the angel conferred upon them the "Priesthood of Aaron," whereupon (2) they baptized each other, and (3) they subsequently ordained each other to the Aaronic Priesthood—but not to the office of priest or teacher. See *Times and Seasons* 3, no. 19 (1 August 1842): 865-866.

35. *BM, 1830*, "The Book of Alma, the Son of Alma," chapter X, page 265.

36. *Painesville Telegraph* (19 April 1831).

37. *BM, 1830*, "The Book of Moroni," chapter II and III, pp. 574-575.

the term disciple to those possessing this authority,[38] but later in 1829 switched to apostle.[39] In a revelation dated 6 April 1830 (the day the church was formally organized), both Smith and Cowdery were called apostles and elders.[40] Two months later the first General Conference of the new church was held, at which time licenses were given to two teachers, three priests, and five elders.[41] Two of those licenses are known still to exist. That of Joseph Smith, Sr., states that "he is a Priest of this Church of Christ,"[42] while that of John Whitmer says "he is an Apostle of Jesus Christ, an Elder of this Church of Christ."[43] A year later the revised "Articles and Covenants" used the same terminology, referring both to Smith and Cowdery as "an apostle of Jesus Christ, an elder of the Church." It further clarified the dual nomenclature by stating that "an apostle is an elder."[44] William McLellin later explained that "an Apostle is not an administrative officer. When they ministered they did it as Elders."[45] That apostles existed in

---

38. *BC* XV: 28.
39. "The Articles of the Church of Christ," in Woodford, 290, refers to Cowdery as "an Apostle of the Lord Jesus Christ by the will of God the Father & the Lord Jesus Christ."
40. *BC* XXII: 1, 13, 14.
41. Donald Q. Cannon and Lyndon W. Cook, eds., *Far West Record: Minutes of the Church of Jesus Christ of Latter-day Saints, 1830-1844* (Salt Lake City, Utah: Deseret Books, 1983), 1; hereafter abbreviated *Far West Record*.
42. Original in LDS Archives; photocopy of original reproduced in Donald Q. Cannon, "Licensing in the Early Church," *Brigham Young University Studies* 22, no. 1 (Winter 1982): 97.
43. Photograph of John Whitmer license, RLDS Library-Archives, Whitmer Papers, P10, f1.
44. *Painesville Telegraph* (19 April 1831).
45. William E. McLellin to Joseph Smith III (July 1872), RLDS

the church as early as 1829 and that twelve apostles may have been selected as early as 1830 is further suggested by the following sources:

First, David Marks, an itinerant preacher, stayed in the home of the Whitmer family on 29 March 1830, just eight days before the church was organized. In his memoirs, published in 1831, he said of his conversation with the Whitmers, "they further stated, that twelve apostles were to be appointed, who would soon confirm their mission by miracles."[46]

Second, an article in *The Cleveland Herald*, dated 25 November 1830, said that because the Book of Mormon "would not sell unless an excitement and curiosity could be raised in the public mind, [the leaders of the new church] have therefore sent out twelve Apostles to promulgate its doctrines, several of whom are in this vicinity expounding its mysteries and baptising converts to its principles...."[47]

Third, in December 1830 letters of introduction were

Archives. Use of the term "apostle" may have carried a connotation of "witness," while "elder" was an officer with administrative responsibilities. Because the Book of Mormon spoke of twelve "disciple/elders," it appears that the total number of apostle/elders in the early months of the Restoration was limited to twelve. As the rapid growth of the movement required more administrative officers, additional elders were called, but without the secondary title of apostle.

46. Mariella Marks, ed., *Memoirs of the Life of David Marks, Minister of the Gospel* (Dove, New Hampshire: Free-Will Baptist Printing Establishment, 1846), 236-237. Note that the first edition was published in 1831.

47. *The Cleveland Herald* (25 November 1830). Although no list of apostles in 1830 is known to exist, a strong case may be made for at least eight men having been called to this position. (1) Joseph Smith and (2) Oliver Cowdery were each called "an apostle of Jesus Christ, an elder of the Church" (*Painesville*

written by Sidney Rigdon in behalf of John Whitmer, calling him "an Apostle of this church"[48]; and by Joseph Smith and John Whitmer in behalf of Orson Pratt (who was ordained an elder on 1 December 1830), calling him "another servant and apostle."[49]

By the end of 1830, however, a change in policy appears to have been made, and new elders were no longer also called apostles.[50] The use of the term de-

---

Telegraph, 19 April 1831). (3) David Whitmer was "called even with that same calling" as the Apostle Paul (*BC* XV: 11). (4) John Whitmer was identified in his license, issued at the General Conference on 9 June 1830, as "an Apostle of Jesus Christ, an Elder of this Church of Christ" (photograph of original license is in the RLDS Library-Archives). (5) Peter Whitmer, (6) Ziba Peterson, and (7) Samuel H. Smith were ordained elders and issued licenses at the same time as John Whitmer; although copies of their licenses are not known to exist, one may assume that they were identical to that of John Whitmer (*Far West Record*, 1). (8) Orson Pratt, in a letter of introduction, was called "another servant and apostle" (see text below). Four other men had been ordained elders before the publication of *The Cleveland Herald* article (Joseph Smith, Sr.; Hyrum Smith; Parley Pratt; and Thomas Marsh). However, there are neither copies of licenses nor other references which refer to these men as apostles (an entry at the end of the 1830 section of the "Journal History" of the LDS Church, copies of which are at the LDS Archives and the Marriott Library of the University of Utah, states that these four men were ordained elders on or before 30 September 1830).

48. E. D. Howe, *Mormonism Unvailed, or, A Faithful Account of that Singular Imposition and Delusion, From its Rise to the Present Time* (Painesville, Ohio: n.p., 1834), 110. This book was reprinted in 1977 by AMS Press, Inc., New York, as part of its series, "Communal Societies in America."

49. From the Newel Knight journal, quoted in William G. Hartley, *They Are My Friends: A History of the Joseph Knight Family, 1825-1850* (Provo, Utah: Grandin Books, 1986), 60.

50. For example, the license of Edward Partridge, who was ordained an elder on 15 December 1830, states simply that he was

clined quickly. By 1835, when the Quorum of Twelve Apostles was organized, no mention was made of the earlier apostles.

Another development at the end of 1830 proved to be of even greater impact on the new church and was initiated by the baptism of a former Campbellite preacher and bishop, Sidney Rigdon. Having been converted in Kirtland, Ohio, by four missionaries sent to the "borders of the Lamanites," Rigdon was convinced that these men had authority from God but was troubled by their apparent inability to prophesy and heal. Blaming Cowdery "for attempting to work miracles" and saying that "it was not intended to be confirmed in that way,"[51] Rigdon went east to meet and influence Joseph Smith.

"ordained as an Elder," with no mention of the word "apostle." See Orson F. Whitney, "Aaronic Priesthood," *The Contributor* 6, no. 1 (October 1884): 5. However, a letter from Ezra Booth to Reverend Eddy, dated 21 November 1831, suggests that, although no new apostles were being designated, a defined group of twelve apostles still existed by late 1831: "And thus by commandment, poor Ziba [Peterson], one of the twelve Apostles, is thrust down; while Oliver the scribe, also an Apostle, who had been guilty of similar conduct, is set on high" (*Painesville Telegraph*, 6 December 1831). Furthermore, a revelation dated 23 September 1832 and addressed to "Eleven high Priests save one" who "are present this day" stated that "you are mine Apostles even Gods high Priests," outlined their duties in preaching the gospel and repeatedly compared these men to the ancient apostles (*Joseph Smith's Kirtland Revelation Book* [Salt Lake City, Utah: Modern Microfilm Co., 1979; hereafter abbreviated *KRB*], 20-31; see also *DC, 1835*, Section IV. The Modern Microfilm publication is a photographic reproduction of the "Kirtland Revelation Book," the original of which is in the LDS Archives).

51. See articles in the *Palmyra Reflector* (14 February and 9 March 1831) and the *Painesville Telegraph* (15 February 1831).

Phase III: December 1830 to November 1831—"High Priesthood"

Rigdon's influence on Joseph Smith was immediate and favorable. Within days of his arrival in New York, his status within the Restoration was declared by revelation: "Behold, verily, verily, I say unto my servant Sidney, I have looked upon thee and thy works. I have heard thy prayers and prepared thee for a greater work. Thou are blessed, for thou shalt do great things. Behold thou was sent forth, even as John, to prepare the way before me, and before Elijah which should come, and thou knew it not."[52] Several days later, with Rigdon as his scribe, Smith received another revelation in which the qualifications for the ministry were changed. The church was directed to move to Ohio, where the elders would "be endowed with power from on high"—something Rigdon had concluded to be lacking in the missionaries who had converted him, but who had failed in their attempts to work miracles—and thus be prepared to "go forth among all nations."[53] Using the terminology of the Gospel of Luke, chapter 24, the revelation likened the Restoration elders to the ancient apostles, who were told by the resurrected Christ that, although they had already been ordained to the ministry, yet they lacked something essential to their forthcoming missions, namely "power from on high." Not until they were endowed with that power on the subsequent Day of Pentecost could they leave Jerusalem on their missions. The nature of the new "endowment"—how and when it would be given, and of

---

52. *BC* XXXVII: 3-6.
53. *BC* XL: 28.

what it would consist—was not described in this revelation but gradually developed over the next five months.

Two February revelations gave additional insights into the endowment. The first stated the necessity of personal preparation on the part of the recipients.[54] The second reinforced the similarity between the modern and ancient elders by promising a pentecostal experience in their new gathering place in Ohio: "I will pour out my spirit upon them in the day that they assemble themselves together."[55] The same revelation directed that all the elders be informed of the assembly, which would be held in Kirtland the first week of June.

Shortly after receiving this revelation, Smith, with Rigdon acting as his scribe, revised the fourteenth chapter of Genesis, which contains one of two Old Testament references to Melchizedek. They added sixteen verses defining an ancient order to which Melchizedek had been ordained as a high priest and through which he had possessed tangible power, a "here and now" type of power that could break mountains, divide seas, dry up waters, and put at defiance the armies of nations.[56]

In May, an unpublished revelation through Smith to Ezra Thayre stated:

> Let my servant Ezra humble himself and at the conference meeting he shall be ordained unto power from on high and he shall go from thence (if he be obedient unto my commandments) and proclaim my gospel unto the

---

54. *BC* XLV: 16.
55. *BC* XLVI: 2.
56. For a comparison of the Authorized (King James) text and the "Inspired Version" produced by Joseph Smith, see *Joseph*

western regions with my servants that must go forth even unto the borders by the Lamanites for behold I have a great work for them to do and it shall be given unto you to know what ye shall do at the conference meeting even so amen.[57]

This revelation linked for the first time the endowment of "power from on high" to ordination,[58] though not yet specifying that the ordination would be to the "order" which had given Melchizedek tangible power. That the elders expected to receive great power at the conference, and that their expectation was public knowledge was verified by an Ohio newspaper article published at the time of the Thayre revelation: "In June they are all to meet, and hold a kind of jubilee in this new 'land of promise,' where they are to work divers

---

Smith's "New Translation" of the Bible (Independence, Missouri: Herald Publishing House, 1970), 78. This chapter of Genesis was revised by Smith and Rigdon between 1 February and 8 March 1831 (see Robert J. Matthews, "A Plainer Translation": Joseph Smith's Translation of the Bible, A History and Commentary [Provo, Utah: Brigham Young University Press, 1975], 96). While the Book of Mormon spoke of Melchizedek being a high priest and taking upon himself "the High Priesthood forever," it did not link tangible power to his priesthood, nor did the King James version of Genesis 14 (see BM, 1830, "The Book of Alma, the Son of Alma," chapter X, page 260). David Whitmer later became adamant in claiming that the introduction of the office of high priest was Sidney Rigdon's doing (see, for example, Whitmer's letter to Joseph Smith III in Saints' Herald 34 [1887]: 92-93). While it is true that Rigdon, in his position as Smith's scribe during this period, would have had ample opportunity to discuss his views with Smith, the fact that the concept of "High Priesthood" and the office of high priest were in the Book of Mormon, which pre-dated Rigdon's contact with Smith, suggests caution in accepting Whitmer's claim.

57. Unpublished revelation, dated May 1831. In KRB, 91-92.
58. Note that the ordination is to be to "power," not to a specified office.

miracles—among others that of raising the dead."[59]

The much anticipated conference began on 3 June 1831 in a Kirtland schoolhouse. On the second day a series of unusual events transpired. Of the many accounts later written of the conference, the most concise was that of John Corrill, the third church historian:

> Previous to this there was a revelation received, requiring the prophet to call the elders together, that they might receive an endowment. This was done, and the meeting took place some time in June. About fifty elders met, which was about all the elders that then belonged to the church. The meeting was conducted by Smith. Some curious things took place. The same visionary and marvellous spirits spoken of before, got hold of some of the elders; it threw one from his seat to the floor; it bound another, so that for some time he could not use his limbs nor speak; and some other curious effects were experienced, but, by a mighty exertion, in the name of the Lord, it was exposed and shown to be from an evil source. The Melchizedek priesthood was then for the first time introduced, and conferred on several of the elders. In this chiefly consisted the endowment—it being a new order—and bestowed authority. However, some doubting took place among the elders, and considerable conversation was held on the subject. The elders not fairly understanding the nature of the endowments, it took some time to reconcile all their feelings.[60]

Other participants who later wrote of the experience included Joseph Smith, Parley P. Pratt, Levi Hancock,

---

59. *Western Courier* (Ravenna, Ohio: 26 May 1831); reprinted in *St. Louis Times* (9 July 1831).
60. John Corrill, *Brief History of the Church of Christ of Latter Day Saints (commonly called Mormons); Including an Account of their Doctrine and Discipline; With the Reasons of the Author for Leaving the Church* (St. Louis, Missouri: printed for the author, 1839), chapter 10.

Lyman Wight, Newel Knight, Ezra Booth, Philo Dibble, and Zebedee Coltrin.[61] An analysis of their accounts leads to several summary comments:

First, it was a pentecost, consisting of revelation, prophecy, vision, healing, casting out of evil spirits, speaking in unknown tongues, and, according to one witness, an unsuccessful attempt to raise a dead child.[62]

---

61. Joseph Smith, "History of Joseph Smith," *Times and Seasons* 5, no. 3 (1 February 1844): 416; Parley P. Pratt, *Autobiography of Parley Parker Pratt* (Salt Lake City, Utah: Deseret Books, 1976), 68; Levi Hancock: "1854 Autobiography," LDS Archives; Lyman Wight: Letter to Wilford Woodruff (24 August 1857), Lyman Wight Letterbook, RLDS Library-Archives (the original letter is in the LDS Archives); Newel Knight: "Autobiographical Sketch," LDS Archives; Ezra Booth: Letter to Reverend Ira Eddy (September 1831), in Howe, 180-190; Philo Dibble, *Juvenile Instructor* 27, no. 10 (15 May 1892): 303; Zebedee Coltrin: "Autobiography," LDS Archives, MC d 2793.

62. Ezra Booth to Rev. Ira Eddy (31 October 1831), in *Painesville Telegraph* (15 November 1831). Booth was ordained to the High Priesthood at the conference (*Far West Record*, 6-7), but left the church a few weeks later. His letters to Rev. Eddy clearly are nonsympathetic toward his former church, and it is tempting to dismiss his account as false. Since all other first-hand witnesses are silent on the subject of attempting to raise the dead child, it is not possible to verify his allegation. However, several pieces of evidence lend credence to his account. First, newspaper articles both before and following the conference described claims by the "Mormonites" that they had power to raise the dead (see *Western Courier*, 26 May 1831; *Niles' Weekly Register*, 16 July 1831; *Vermont Patriot and State Gazette*, 18 September 1831). Second, the death of Joseph Brackenbury, an early Mormon missionary, on 7 March 1832, was followed by a much-publicized and unsuccessful attempt by his fellow elders to raise him from the dead (see *Burlington [Vermont] Sentinel*, 23 March 1832; and reprints of this article in the *Wayne Sentinel* of Palymyra, New York, 11 April 1832, and the *Ohio Star*, 12 April 1832). Two decades later, LDS Church historian George A. Smith

Second, it introduced a new order, into which about half the elders at the conference were inducted by ordination, which was called the Order of Melchizedek, a name derived from the Melchizedek passages of the Book of Mormon and Genesis 14; it was also called the High Priesthood, a term used in the Book of Mormon Melchizedek passages, but not in Genesis.[63] It was *not* the *office* of high priest, even though the Book of Mormon passages had referred to Melchizedek as a high priest. Conference minutes from 4 and 24 August; 1, 6, and 12 September; 10, 11, and 21 October; and 1, 8, 9, 11, and 12-13 November still listed as elders men who had previously been ordained to the High Priesthood.[64] The term "high priest" was not used in conference minutes until 26 April 1832.[65]

Third, it was an endowment of tangible power, such as had not yet been seen within the Restoration. Within weeks of the conference Ezra Booth, although by then dissociated from the movement, acknowledged that the participants professed "to be endowed with the same power as the ancient apostles were."[66] (Thus, the prom-

----

wrote to Brackenbury's widow, asking "the circumstances of his death, burial, and attempted resurrection" (George A. Smith to Elizabeth Brackenbury [29 August 1855], Henry Stebbins Collection, P24/F1, RLDS Library-Archives). Third, when E. D. Howe reprinted the Booth account in 1834, he told of an interview with the parents of the dead child, who said "that they were prevented from procuring medical aid for the child, by the representations of the elders, that it was in no danger—that it would certainly be restored" (Howe, 190).

63. *BM, 1830*, "The Book of Alma, the Son of Alma," chapter X, page 260.
64. *Far West Record*, 9-31.
65. Ibid., 43.
66. Howe, 180-181.

ise of an endowment, contained in revelations beginning in January 1831, was fulfilled at the June conference and not at the time of the dedication of the Kirtland House of the Lord in 1836, as other writers have suggested.[67]) That the endowment conferred extraordinary powers upon the recipients was chronicled most dramatically by Jared Carter. Shortly after the conference a woman belonging to the church fell from a wagon on her way to a meeting and sustained injuries feared to be fatal. Jared wrote:

> In my conversation with her, I told her that she need not have any more pain, and also mentioned my Brother Simeon who was endowed with great power from on high, and that she might be healed, if she had faith. Brother Simeon also conversed with her, and after awhile took her by the hand, saying, "I command you in the name of Jesus Christ to arise and walk." And she arose and walked from room to room.[68]

Finally, it was *not* then termed Melchizedek Priesthood, in spite of what Joseph Smith, Lyman Wight,

67. Hyrum M. Smith and Janne M. Sjodahl, *The Doctrine and Covenants, Containing Revelations Given to Joseph Smith, Jr., The Prophet, With an Introduction and Historical and Exegetical Notes* (Salt Lake City, Utah: Deseret Books, 1960), 208; Sidney B. Sperry, *Doctrine and Covenants Compendium* (Salt Lake City, Utah: Bookcraft, 1960), 159; Joseph Fielding Smith, *Church History and Modern Revelation, Being a Course of Study for the Melchizedek Priesthood Quorums for the Year 1947* (Salt Lake City, Utah: The Council of the Twelve Apostles, Deseret News Press, 1946), 156; Roy W. Doxey, *The Doctrine and Covenants Speaks*, vol. 2 (Salt Lake City, Utah: Deseret Books, 1970), 211; F. Henry Edwards, *A Commentary on the Doctrine and Covenants* (Independence, Missouri: Herald Publishing House, 1967), 140.
68. Jared Carter journal, in "Journal History" (8 June 1831), LDS Archives. Simeon had been ordained to the High Priesthood at the conference, Jared had not (see *Far West Record*, 7).

John Corrill, and Newel Knight later wrote. As will be shown later in this monograph, the term "Melchizedek Priesthood" did not exist within the Restoration until 1835, at which time it became an umbrella term encompassing all prior component terms. All of the accounts of the 1831 conference which used the term "Melchizedek Priesthood" were written after 1835 and inaccurately used a later term to describe an earlier event. Most conference accounts, by contrast, accurately used the terms "High Priesthood" and/or "Order of Melchizedek."[69]

Enthusiasm and expectations were extraordinarily high following the conference as the elders traveled from Kirtland to Independence, Missouri, to dedicate a site for a temple.[70] A national periodical commented that "some of them affect a power even to raise the dead, and perchance, (such is the weakness of human nature), really believe that they can do it!"[71] Yet their arduous journey to and from Missouri resulted in disappointment and lowered expectations. At a conference in Kirtland on 25 October, Joseph Smith introduced a new dimension to the High Priesthood and simultaneously took the first step in the development

---

69. Furthermore, a revelation dated 16 February 1832 refers to "priests of the most high after the order of Melchisedeck," rather than using the later term "Melchizedek Priesthood" (*KRB*, 5; see also *The Evening and the Morning Star* 1, no. 2 [July 1832]: 10-11, and *DC, 1835* XCI:5).

70. A local newspaper reported, "They still persist in their power to work miracles. They say they have often seen them done—the sick are healed—the lame walk—devils are cast out;—and these assertions are made by men heretofore considered rational men, and men of truth" (*Geauga Gazette* [Painesville, Ohio: 21 June 1831]).

71. *Niles' Weekly Register* (16 July 1831).

of the unique Latter Day Saint theology of afterlife by stating "that the order of the High-priesthood is that they have the power given them to seal up the Saints unto eternal life. And said it was the privilege of every Elder present to be ordained to the High priesthood."[72] Before this, authority and power within the Restoration, by whatever title or description, had been "here and now." With this pronouncement the power of the High Priesthood suddenly extended beyond the grave. Within two weeks, elders who had received the High Priesthood exercised their new power, sealing entire congregations "up unto eternal life."[73]

Shortly after the conference, a revelation directed to four men recently ordained to the High Priesthood further defined that priesthood in three ways:

First, it formally established the *office* of high priest. After this, High Priesthood meant the office of high priest, with no further reference to endowment.[74]

Second, it said that the inspired words of high priests were "scripture."

Third, it reaffirmed the authority of the High Priesthood to seal people to eternal life, while adding the caveat that divine confirmation, in advance, was required.[75]

---

72. *Far West Record*, 20-21.
73. Between 9 and 26 November, Reynolds Cahoon participated in three such "sealings." See Reynolds Cahoon diaries, LDS Archives.
74. However, the linkage between endowment and missionary work, which had led to the June conference, remained intact and was the focal point of later Kirtland and Nauvoo "endowments."
75. This revelation probably was intended to be published in *BC*, but the printing press was destroyed by a mob before type was set. The first published version was in *The Evening and the*

Another revelation given simultaneously added a darker dimension to the sealing power of the High Priesthood, declaring that the wicked could, by action of that priesthood, be sealed up to condemnation.[76]

Phase IV: November 1831 to March 1836—Organizational Development

A revelation given in November 1831 initiated a process of organizational development which continued over a period of nearly five years, and which reached a zenith at the dedication of the Kirtland House of the Lord in 1836. To facilitate understanding of this process, it is useful to examine five areas of development within these years:

1. The formation of a centralized church government
2. The organization of officers into functional groups
3. The continual redefining of "priesthood"
4. The further empowerment of elders as a prerequisite to their missionary labors
5. The establishment and development of the office of Patriarch

1. Formation of centralized government

From the time the Latter Day Saint movement began in August 1829,[77] its government was largely democratic. Although Joseph Smith clearly occupied a favored position as the translator of the Book of Mormon

---

Morning Star 1, no. 5 (Octboer 1832): 35. An expanded version was published in *DC, 1835* XXII.

76. *BC* I:2. This revelation was dated 1 November 1831.

77. David Whitmer wrote that this was the date when he, Smith, and Cowdery, the first three elders of the Restoration, began to preach and baptize. By the time of the legal incorporation of the

and as God's spokesman, terms of administrative priority such as "president" or "first Elder" were absent during most of the church's first year.[78] By the time of the first General Conference in June 1830, Smith was called the "first Elder" and Cowdery the "second Elder."[79] It soon became apparent that the growth of the church dictated other administrative changes. One such change was the departure from the precedent of the Book of Mormon and early revelations which stated that only elders could ordain other officers.[80] By 1831 priests were authorized to ordain deacons, teachers, and other priests, perhaps as a concession to overburdening of the few elders in the church at that time.[81]

More significant was a revelation received in November of that year, "regulating the Presidency of the church,"[82] which first outlined both the need for and the structure of a formal presidency:

church on 6 April 1830, there were already three congregations with an aggregate membership of about seventy (*An Address to All Believers in Christ*, 32-33).

78. For example, although the 1835 version of the "Articles and Covenants of the Church" called Smith "the first elder of this Church," all earlier versions of this revelation referred to him simply as "an elder of this church." Compare *Painesville Telegraph* (19 April 1831) and *BC* XXIV:3 to *DC, 1835* II:1.

79. These terms followed the signatures of Joseph Smith and Oliver Cowdery on the licenses of John Whitmer and Joseph Smith, Sr., issued at that conference. Reference to both licenses was made in an earlier section of this monograph.

80. *BM, 1830*, "The Book of Moroni, chapter III; "The Articles of the Church of Christ," in Woodford, 288; *BC* XV: 35.

81. The earliest known account of this change was "The Articles and Covenants of the Church of Christ," in the *Painesville Telegraph* (19 April 1831).

82. This revelation, although received in November 1831 (see *KRB*, 84-86), was not published until 1835, when it was included in an expanded revelation dated 28 March 1835 (*DC, 1835* III).

1. "Wherefore it must needs be that one be appointed of the high Priesthood to preside over the Priesthood, and he shall be called President of the high priesthood of the Church, or in other words the presiding high Priest over the high priesthood of the Church."

2. More than a figurehead, this president would hold the power to authorize all other officers within the church to administer "ordinances and blessings upon the church by the laying on of hands."

3. He would also serve a judicial role, as president of the court of the High Priesthood, "the highest court in the church," thus bringing the informal church judicial system under central control.[83]

4. As a final endorsement of the sweeping powers granted to the new position, the revelation concluded by stating that "the duty of the President of the office of

---

83. Judicial matters had been addressed informally as early as 1830 in a revelation calling upon the teachers to "see that there is no iniquity in the church." (The earliest known version of this revelation which describes this duty of teachers was published in the *Painesville Telegraph* [19 April 1831].) The following year, elders (preferably in the presence of the newly called bishop) were empowered to judge church members accused of adultery or fornication (*BC* XLVII, dated February 1831). The role of bishop was expanded by a revelation dated 1 August 1831 "to be a judge in Israel, like as it was in ancient days" (*BC* LIX: 21) without the assistance of elders. The November 1831 revelation designating the president as chief judicial officer also authorized him to call twelve counselors if he chose, and thus set the pattern for the formation of high councils two and a half years later. George A. Smith later said, "There had been several Councils of twelve High Priests called for special cases, but they organized it permanently on the 17th Feb 1834" (*Journal of Discourses* 11:7 [15 November 1864]).

the high Priesthood is to preside over the whole and to be like unto Moses."[84]

Two months later, at a conference in Ohio on 24 January 1832, Joseph Smith was "acknowledged President of the High Priesthood," and formally ordained to that office by Sidney Rigdon. At the same time, Rigdon "ordained" Orson Pratt, who was already an elder, to "preside over the Elders," thus underscoring the recent distinction between the offices of elder and high priest.[85]

Simultaneously, a second conference in Independence, Missouri, moved toward centralized control of all ordinations, unanimously resolving "that there be no person ordained in the churches in the land of Zion to the office of Elder Priest Teacher or Deacon without the united voice of the Church in writing in which such individual resides."[86]

---

84. The phrase "preside over the whole" was changed to "preside over the whole church" when the revelation was published in 1835 (DC, 1835 III:42).

85. Orson Pratt journal (25 January 1832) in Elden J. Watson, ed., The Orson Pratt Journals (Salt Lake City, Utah: Elden J. Watson, 1975), 11. See also HC 1: 243. Although this act appears to have presaged the later formation of "quorums" of elders, Pratt's ordination to the High Priesthood only one week later delayed for years the emergence of organized, functional groups of elders. See Lyndon W. Cook, The Revelations of the Prophet Joseph Smith [Provo, Utah: Seventy's Mission Bookstore, 1981], 49, for the dating of Pratt's ordination to the High Priesthood.)

86. Minutes of a conference in Independence, Missouri (23-24 January 1832); contained in a letter from Oliver Cowdery to Joseph Smith (28 January 1832). Photograph of the original letter is in the RLDS Library-Archives, Miscellany, P19, f4. This was later amended such that ordination to the higher offices of priesthood, elder, and high priest required the consent of a conference of high priests rather than the voice of the General Church (see Far West Record, 28 August 1833).

The consolidation of centralized authority was strengthened several weeks later with the selection and ordination of Jesse Gause and Sidney Rigdon as Smith's "councellors of the ministry of the presidency of the high Priesthood."[87] An unpublished revelation given to Bishop Newel K. Whitney the same month reaffirmed the primacy of the "presidency of the high Priesthood" in "all the concerns of the church."[88]

Nearly two years passed before the next significant step in the process of centralization. Having seen, in vision, the manner in which ancient church councils were organized, Joseph Smith convened a conference in Kirtland on 17 February 1834 and organized "the high council of the Church of Christ," consisting of twelve high priests.[89] Strictly judicial in function, the high council exercised both original and appellate jurisdiction.[90] Although delegating substantial powers to this body, Smith signalled the continuity of strong, centralized control by placing himself and his two counselors at its head.

In recognition of the growth of the church beyond the two centers of gathering (Kirtland and Independence), provision was made at this conference for *ad hoc* councils, patterned after the Kirtland High Council, to settle

---

87. *KRB*, 10-11.
88. Unpublished revelation (March 1832); Newel K. Whitney papers, Special Collections, Harold B. Lee Library, Brigham Young University.
89. "Kirtland High Council Minutes" (17 February 1834); original in LDS Archives. (See also *KRB*, 111-115, and *DC, 1835* V.)
90. Ibid. The draft version of the minutes had placed the high council subordinate to the bishop's court, but the amended version authorized the High Council to settle "important difficulties...which could not be settled by the Church, or the bishop's council to the satisfaction of the parties."

"the most difficult cases of church matters" abroad. These councils would be temporary, and subordinate to the Standing High Council, which could, upon appeal, reverse their decisions.

One week later, a revelation called on Joseph Smith to lead an expedition (known as "Zion's Camp") from Ohio to Missouri, to rescue the persecuted church members and thus "redeem Zion."[91] Although the mission failed to redeem Zion and several members of the expedition died of cholera, Smith did succeed in organizing a high council while he was in Missouri.[92] Four days later he confidently stated "that he had lived to see the Church of Jesus Christ established on earth according to the order of heaven; and should he now be taken from this body of people, the work of the Lord would roll on."[93]

Smith's conclusion that the church organization was now complete proved to be short-lived. After returning to Kirtland, he met with the Young brothers, Brigham and Joseph, and related to them a vision he had experienced while praying to know the fate of those who had died on the expedition. He said, "Brethren, I have seen those men who died of the cholera in our camp; and the Lord knows, if I get a mansion as bright as theirs, I ask no more."[94] Then, apparently drawing from

91. *KRB*, 108-111, revelation dated 24 February 1834; see also *DC*, *LDS* 103.
92. *Far West Record* (3 July 1834).
93. Lyman Wight diary (7 July 1834), in *The History of the Reorganized Church of Jesus Christ of Latter Day Saints*, Volume 1 (Independence, Missouri: Herald Publishing House, 1967), 515-516; see also *Far West Record* (7 July 1834).
94. Joseph Young, Sr., *History of the Organization of the Seventies* (Salt Lake City, Utah: Deseret News Steam Printing Establishment, 1878), 1.

the same vision, he outlined the formation of the final two bodies of centralized authority, the Twelve Apostles and the Seventy.[95] The following Saturday, 14 February 1835, the Twelve were appointed; two weeks later, the First Quorum of Seventy was chosen. Nearly all the men in both groups had proven their dedication by serving in Zion's Camp.

Although the initial mission of the Twelve was "to open the door of the gospel to foreign nations," with the Seventy "under their direction to follow in their tracks,"[96] it soon became apparent that missions other than proselytizing awaited the Twelve. Two weeks after organizing the Twelve, Smith told them that they were also to be a "traveling high council, who are to preside over all the churches of the Saints among the Gentiles, where there is no presidency established"[97]—that is, everywhere except Kirtland and Independence, where standing high councils presided.

That the Twelve, or "Traveling High Council," would ultimately overshadow the standing high councils may have been indicated by a revelation, given through Smith at the request of the Twelve, on 28 March 1835.[98] While stating that four councils (the Twelve Apostles, the Seventy, the combined Standing High Councils of the Stakes of Zion [of which there was but one, Kirtland, at the time], and the Standing High Council in Zion

---

95. A revelation dated the following month stated that the Seventy had been organized "according to the vision," although it gave no further information regarding the vision (*DC, 1835* III: 43; see also *HC* 2:201-202).

96. Young, 2, 14.

97. "Kirtland High Council Minutes," 88; quoted in D. Michael Quinn, "The Evolution of the Presiding Quorums of the LDS Church," *Journal of Mormon History* 1 (1974): 27.

98. *HC* 2: 210.

[Independence]) all had "authority and power" equal to that of the First Presidency, the listing first of the Twelve suggested a favored status.[99] Furthermore, to the Twelve was given the exclusive authority "to ordain and set in order all the other officers of the church."[100] By August 1835 the revelation which had established the standing high councils was changed in a way to give further priority to the Twelve: whereas decisions of the standing high councils (and of the *ad hoc* councils of traveling high priests) could still be appealed, those of the Twelve could not.[101]

By late 1835, then, the centralization of authority was complete. Ordinations were under central control,[102] church members in the stakes and in Zion were under the control of the standing high councils and bishops, and those outside of Zion and the stakes came under the jurisdiction of the Twelve Apostles and the Seventy. All of these bodies, in turn, answered to the president (Joseph Smith), who was "to preside over the whole church, and to be like unto Moses."[103] Although changes would yet be made in the responsibilities of these governing bodies (the most significant being the ascendancy of the Twelve to being the sole central

---

99. *DC, 1835* III: 12-15.
100. *DC, 1835* III: 30.
101. *DC, 1835* V: 13.
102. The third historian of the church, John Corrill, wrote: "For some time after the commencement of the church, an elder might ordain an elder, priest, teacher, or deacon, when and where he thought proper, but, after Stakes were planted, and the church became organized, they established a rule that none should be ordained without consent of the church or branch that he belonged to; neither should any man be placed over a branch or take charge of it without consent of same" (Corrill, chapter 13).
103. *DC, 1835* III: 42.

governing body of the church following Smith's death), no new units of ecclesiastical government would be added during the remaining nine years of Smith's ministry.

2. Organization of functional groups of officers

In the earliest days of the Restoration, only three offices existed: teachers, priests, and elder/apostles. Teachers and priests were ordained without regard to number or organization; elder/apostles, though initially a defined group of twelve men (judging from contemporary accounts), did not function as a unit. Each office had a job description, with the recipients of its ministry being church members in general. In November 1831 the same revelation that had initiated the process of centralization by calling for the selection of a president also mandated the organizing of each office into well-defined groups. Deacons[104] were to be organized into groups of twelve; teachers, twenty-four; priests, forty-eight; and elders, ninety-six. Each group was to be presided over by a president holding the same office. More importantly, this revelation called for the president of each group to act as a shepherd over his flock, "to sit in council with them and to teach them

---

104. The office of deacon did not exist either in the Book of Mormon nor in the early Restoration. For example, as late as February 1831, a revelation listing the offices in the church listed only elders, priests, and teachers (*BC* XLIV: 13). The earliest known mention of deacons was in the "Articles and Covenants of the Church," published in the *Painesville Telegraph* (19 April 1831).

their duty edifying one another as it is given according to the covenants."[105]

Although the blueprint for group function had been drawn, no group was able to respond effectively at the time. Indeed, by the time of the completion of the Kirtland House of the Lord in 1836, only the teachers had established a significant tradition of group function.[106]

3. Redefining of "priesthood"

As shown earlier, the concept of dual levels of authority was present in the Book of Mormon and formed the model for the Restoration, with both levels having been restored in 1829. However, neither layer was named at that time, nor had a hierarchical relationship been specified among the offices within each layer. Through mid-1832 the only use of the word "priesthood" had been in conjunction with "high priesthood," which had first referred to an order of elders, then to the office of high priest.

---

105. *KRB*, 84-86. Although the term "quorum" would not be applied to these groups for several years, the concept established by this revelation remains the guiding principle in LDS and RLDS priesthood quorum function today.

106. The earliest known record of such function began on Christmas Day, 1834. See "Teachers Quorum Minute Book" (December 25, 1834-February 12, 1845), MS 3428, LDS Archives. In an effort to complete preparations for the March 1836 Solemn Assembly and endowment, "the quorums of the Church were organized in the presence of the Church, and commenced confessing their faults and asking forgiveness" (Oliver Cowdery diary [17 January 1836]; in Leonard J. Arrington, "Oliver Cowdery's Kirtland, Ohio, 'Sketch Book,'" *Brigham Young University Studies* 12, no. 4 (1972): 416.

A revelation in September 1832 expanded the use of the word "priesthood" and for the first time made some offices subordinate to others.[107] This revelation is somewhat confusing, for it deals with three terms—holy priesthood, high priesthood, and lesser priesthood—the first two of which have since been used interchangeably. Furthermore, the revelation was given to two groups of men over a two-day period (seven elders on 22 September and "[e]leven high Priests save one" the following day), and for two separate purposes ("explaining the two priesthoods" and "commissioning the Apostles to preach the gospel"[108]). The absence of the original manuscript of the revelation makes it impossible to identify with certainty the "seam" connecting the two parts.

The revelation begins by describing a "holy priesthood" (the first time this term was used within the Restoration) which Moses received from his father-in-law, Jethro, and which had descended lineally from Adam through Melchizedek, "which priesthood continueth in the church of God, in all generations."[109] It then describes a second "priesthood" which the Lord had confirmed "upon Aaron and his seed" that "continueth and abideth forever, with the priesthood which is after the holiest order of God."[110] While referring to two levels of priesthood, the revelation does not clarify how these two correspond to the three events of 1829 (lower and higher authority) and 1831 (high priest-

107. DC, 1835 IV; see also KRB, 20-31.
108. KRB, index.
109. DC, 1835 IV: 2.
110. DC, 1835 IV: 3.

hood). Clarification comes from Smith's diary, written at the same time this revelation was received, in which he recounts the early events of the Restoration:[111]

1. "firstly he receiving the testamony from on high"

2. "seccondly the ministering of Angels"

3. "thirdly the reception of the holy Priesthood by the ministring of Aangels to administer the letter of the Gospel—the Law and commandments as they were given unto him—and the ordinencs"

4. "forthly a confirmation and reception of the high Priesthood after the holy order of the son of the living God power and ordinence from on high to preach the gospel in the administration and demonstration of the spirit."[112]

Comparison of the autobiography to the revelation shows that the term "holy priesthood" was being used synonymously with the higher authority conferred in June 1829 for the following reasons:

- First, its reception pre-dated that of the "high priest-hood" (June 1831).
- Second, it was associated with the ministering of angels (later named as Peter, James, and John).
- Third, it held responsibility for the "administration of the Gospel" and "the ordinances," both defined within the revelation as part of the greater "holy priest-hood."[113]

---

111. Dean Jessee dates the diary entry between 20 July and 27 November 1832; the revelation is dated 22-23 September 1832. See Dean C. Jessee, *The Personal Writings of Joseph Smith* (Salt Lake City, Utah: Deseret Books, 1984), 640, footnote 6.

112. Ibid., 4.

113. The silence of the diary relative to the second, lesser priesthood must be noted. While it is possible that Smith included the "lesser" as part of the "greater" in his diary, and that "Aangels"

Similarly, the diary account of the reception of the high priesthood fits the 1831 record, rather than the events of 1829, for the following reasons:

- First, its reception post-dated that of the "holy priesthood."
- Second, it was *not* associated with angelic intervention.
- Third, it associated the high priesthood with "power...from on high to preach the Gospel."

The use of the term "high priesthood" in this revelation,[114] therefore, refers to the *office* of high priest and not to the higher authority of Peter, James, and John. This office, according to the revelation, is superior to its two appendages, the offices of elder and bishop. Similarly, the "lesser priesthood," that is, the office of priest or "lesser priest" (verse 22 of the same revelation) is superior to its two appendages, the offices of teacher and deacon.[115]

In summary, the revelation on priesthood of September 1832 applied for the first time the word "priesthood" to each of the two levels of authority restored in 1829. While not yet using the later term "Aaronic Priesthood" to refer to the authority restored by John the Baptist on 15 May 1829, it moved in that direction by associ-

---

could refer to John the Baptist *in addition to* Peter, James, and John, the points of concordance between the diary and the revelation deal with the authority restored by the three apostles, not the authority restored by John the Baptist. It is also possible that Smith included the lesser priesthood in the "ministering of Angels," but there is insufficient evidence to make this point conclusively.

114. *DC, 1835* IV: 5.
115. Ibid. Adding to the confusion, a later portion of this revelation, known as the "oath and covenant" of the priesthood, refers first to "these two priesthoods" (i.e., those of Moses/Peter, James,

ating such priesthood with "Aaron and his seed." Similarly, the authority restored by Peter, James, and John was also called "priesthood," and while the later term "Melchizedek Priesthood" was not yet used, the connection between this priesthood and Melchizedek was firmly established. The relationship between offices, while perhaps implied in earlier records, was now made explicit: lesser priests and high priests were dominant, with teachers and deacons subordinate to the former and elders and bishops to the latter.

Before the time of this revelation, there had been no indication that ordination to an office (or a level of authority) was a right. By stating that the lesser priesthood had been conferred upon "Aaron and his seed throughout all their generation," this revelation became the starting point for a doctrine of priesthood-through-lineage. Several weeks later this doctrine was formalized in a revelation stating that "ye are lawful heirs according to the flesh," and that "the Priesthood hath remained and must needs remain through you and your lineage untill the restoration of all things...."[116]

The next step in defining priesthood came through a revelation in March 1835.[117] This revelation marked the introduction of the two terms, "Aaronic Priesthood" and "Melchizedek Priesthood," which have since been used

---

and John, and Aaron/John the Baptist), then merely to "the priesthood," apparently a generic reference to both (see verse 6).

116. *DC, 1835* VI: 3 (6 December 1832).

117. *DC, 1835* III. As was noted earlier, this revelation consists of two parts, the first from November 1831, the second dated 28 March 1835. The revelation, as published in *DC, 1835* and subsequent editions of the Doctrine and Covenants does not indicate that many of the verses are from the earlier revelation, which is in the *KRB*, 84-86, but which was never published in its 1831

by all Latter Day Saint churches to refer to formal authority. In contrast to the revelation on priesthood of September 1832, this revelation used the word "priesthood" in a strictly generic sense (as is still the case today), referring to all officers within each of the two levels of authority, rather than to a specific office. Thus, whereas the 1832 revelation had teachers and deacons as appendages to the "lesser priesthood"—i.e., the *office* of priest—the three offices of priest, teacher, and deacon were now part of the Aaronic Priesthood—which, in turn, served an "umbrella" function, referring to no specific office. Similarly, the offices of elder and high priest were now part of the Melchizedek Priesthood (which now referred to no specific office), rather than elders being appendages to high priests, as the earlier revelation had outlined. Finally, the office of bishop, which previously had been an appendage to the High Priesthood, was now part of the Aaronic Priesthood.[118]

Shortly after the receipt of this revelation, the collected revelations were assembled and edited for publication as *Doctrine and Covenants of the Church of the Latter Day Saints*. Among the editorial changes was an addition to a revelation dated September 1830. Whereas the earlier form of the revelation was silent

---

format. All of the material referenced in this portion of this monograph is from the 1835 portion of the revelation.

118. The office of seventy was introduced in the 1835 revelation but was not specifically placed under the umbrella of Melchizedek Priesthood, unlike elders and high priests. This suggests that the verses relating to seventies were from a third revelation. Further evidence supporting this hypothesis comes from verse 43: "And it is according to the vision, showing the order of the seventy," a vision not described in this or any other known revelation.

regarding angelic intervention in the restoration of authority, the new version described John the Baptist as the messenger who restored the "first priesthood," while Peter, James, and John were named as restorers of the apostleship, this being the first time that the ancient apostles had explicitly been linked to the June 1829 restoration.[119] The use of the word "apostles" rather than "Melchizedek Priesthood" was significant, for while apostleship formed a part of Melchizedek Priesthood, the latter term, by the time of its adoption in 1835, encompassed much more than just the apostleship. It is unfortunate that this distinction did not remain clear. After 1835, references to earlier events, including those of June 1829 and June 1831, frequently made use of the term "Melchizedek Priesthood." The failure of later commentators to understand the anachronism led to elaborate gyrations in an attempt to deal with such statements as "I was also present with Joseph when the higher or Melchizedek priesthood was restored by the holy angels of God [in 1829],"[120] and "the Melchizedek priesthood was then [June 1831] for the first time introduced."[121]

---

119. *DC, 1835* L: 2-3.
120. Oliver Cowdery (17 October 1848); quoted by Reuben Miller in *Millennial Star* 21, no. 34 (20 August 1859): 544.
121. Corrill, chapter 10 (written in 1839). In editing Joseph Smith's history for publication, B. H. Roberts devoted a lengthy footnote to a discussion of the "apparent" problem of the Melchizedek Priesthood having been restored at the June 1831 conference, rather than in 1829. He concluded, incorrectly, that the accounts meant to describe the restoration of the *office* of high priest (*History of the Church of Jesus Christ of Latter-day Saints* 1: 176). In dealing with the same dilemma, RLDS Apostle Heman C. Smith concluded, again incorrectly, that the accounts placing the restoration of the Melchizedek Priesthood in 1831 actually

4. Empowerment of missionaries

The central purpose of the gathering in Ohio in 1831 and the June conference in the same year had been the endowment of the elders with "power from on high" such that they, as the ancient apostles, be prepared to spread the message of the Gospel. Within months of the 1831 endowment, however, its relevance to missionary work seems to have lessened. There was no repeat of a pentecostal experience for elders who had not attended the June conference, nor was it mandatory thereafter that elders be ordained to the High Priesthood before embarking on their missionary journeys.[122]

Near the end of 1832, when several missionaries had returned from their travels, Joseph Smith received a revelation indicating that further preparation was required of the missionaries, "that ye may be prepared in all things when I shall send you again."[123] This prepa-

---

"had reference to the *fullness* of the Melchisedec priesthood being bestowed for the *first time* in June, 1831" (*The History of the Reorganized Church of Jesus Christ of Latter Day Saints* 1: 193; emphasis in original). As will be shown later, the "fullness of the Melchisedec priesthood" was not restored until 1843. Had they both followed the simple rule of evaluating each account on the basis of when it was *written*, rather than the date of the event of which it writes, and compensated for the anachronistic terminology accordingly, the apparent discrepancies would have been resolved.

122. For example, Samuel H. Smith and Orson Hyde were appointed on 25 January 1832 to serve a mission to the Eastern States. Smith had received the endowment at the June 1831 conference, while Hyde had not. Yet Hyde, in his missionary diary, never mentioned Smith's endowment, never mentioned that he, himself, had not received it, and nowhere indicated that his position as a missionary was subordinate to Smith's.

123. *DC, 1835* VII: 21; see also *KRB*, 33-48.

ration was to be both spiritual ("sanctify yourselves; yea purify your hearts"—verse 20) and intellectual ("teach one another the doctrine of the kingdom...of things both in heaven, and in the earth"—verse 21). To facilitate the preparation Smith was commanded to establish a school for the elders (verse 36).

The opening of the "School of the Prophets" occurred on 23-24 January 1833. Although never referred to as an "endowment," the school's opening bore a remarkable resemblance to the 1831 endowment:

- First, its sole purpose was the preparation of the elders for further missionary labors.
- Second, it required the gathering of the elders at a designated place and time.
- Third, it marked the introduction of an ordinance. Whereas the ordinance in 1831 had been ordination to the High Priesthood, this time it was the washing of the feet by the president (Joseph Smith), in similitude of the gesture of Jesus to his apostles.
- Finally, it was accompanied by a pentecostal outpouring, including speaking in tongues, prophesying, and "many manifestations of the holy spirit."[124]

As had been the case in 1831, the pentecostal outpouring was not repeated with subsequent admissions of elders to the school. However, the expectation that it would be required of elders that they gain "power from

---

124. Zebedee Coltrin diary (24 January 1833), LDS Archives. The most detailed accounts of the opening of the School of the Prophets are the Coltrin diary; the "Kirtland High Council Minutes" (23 January 1833), LDS Archives; and Lucy Mack Smith's manuscript history, 162-163, LDS Archives (photocopy of manuscript in author's possession).

on high" through their participation in the school was underscored in a letter written by Oliver Cowdery the following year:

> God has appointed a school for his faithful Elders: In it they are to be taught *all* things necessary to qualify them for their ministry: In it they are to learn: In it they are to be endowed with power from on high: but when entrusted with the great office and authority to preach and are sent out, it is with the expectation and consideration they will do so.[125]

Coincident with the decision to build the Kirtland House of the Lord was the coupling of the ideas of "endowment" and "sacred space." A revelation in June 1833 stated: "I gave unto you a commandment, that you should build an house, in the which house I design to endow those whom I have chosen with power from on high."[126] The same sentiment was stated more forcefully a year later by Oliver Cowdery:

> We want you to understand that the Lord has not promised to endow his servants from on high only on the condition that they build him a house; and if the house is not built the Elders will not be endowed with power, and if they are not they can never go to the nations with the everlasting gospel.[127]

Several weeks later, during the return from the Zion's Camp expedition, Smith received a revelation which

---

125. Oliver Cowdery (Kirtland, Ohio) to J. G. Fosdick (Pontiac, Michigan) (4 February 1834), Oliver Cowdery letterbook, 25-26, Huntington Library.
126. *DC, 1835* XCV: 2 (revelation dated 1 June 1833).
127. Oliver Cowdery (Kirtland, Ohio) to John F. Boynton (Saco, Maine) (6 May 1834), Oliver Cowdery letterbook, 45-46, Huntington Library.

added a dimension to the anticipated endowment by stating that the redemption of Zion "cannot be brought to pass until mine elders are endowed with power from on high; for, behold, I have prepared a greater endowment and blessing to be poured out upon them."[128]

During the winter of 1835-1836, the elders worked to complete the House of the Lord and to prepare themselves for the anticipated endowment.[129] The dedication of the building occurred on 27 March 1836 and involved the general church membership. Three days later, in the same building, a "solemn assembly" was conducted, which involved only the adult males and which constituted the anticipated endowment. As had been the case in 1831 and 1833, the 1836 endowment was pentecostal:

> The brethren continued exhorting, prophesying and speaking in tongues until 5 o clock in the morning—the Saviour made his appearance to some, while angels minestered unto others, and it was a penticost and enduement indeed, long to be remembered.[130]

----

128. *KRB*, 97-100 (revelation dated 22 June 1834). It is significant that the phrase "greater endowment" was used, apparently a reference to the 1831 endowment whose power clearly had been insufficient to redeem Zion. Without explanation, the word "great" was substituted for "greater" in published versions of this revelation.

129. In addition to preparing oneself spiritually, it was necessary that one's body be washed and anointed and that the feet be washed in a manner similar to that used in the opening of the School of the Prophets in 1833. The best descriptions of the preparations during the winter of 1835-1836 are found in the diaries of Joseph Smith (see Faulring) and Oliver Cowdery (see Arrington).

130. Joseph Smith diary (30 March 1836), in Scott H. Faulring, ed., *An American Prophet's Record: The Diaries and Journals of Joseph Smith* (Salt Lake City, Utah: Signature Books in association with Smith Research Associates, 1989), 155.

Having received the required empowerment, the elders subsequently embarked on missions to carry the gospel to all nations, the first being the British Isles in 1837.

5. Patriarchal priesthood and patriarchal blessings

On 18 December 1833 Joseph Smith gathered his family and gave them blessings. In blessing his father, he said:

> He shall be called a prince over his posterity, holding the keys of the patriarchal priesthood over the kingdom of God on earth, even the Church of the Latter Day Saints; and he shall sit in the general assembly of patriarchs, even in council with the Ancient of Days when he shall sit and all the patriarchs with him—and shall enjoy his right and authority under the direction of the Ancient of Days.[131]

While the term "patriarchal priesthood" would be used a decade later in a markedly different context,[132] its use in 1833 appears simply to have referred to the *office* of patriarch, even as the terms "lesser priesthood" and "high priesthood," as used at this same time, referred to the respective offices of lesser priest and high

---

131. Patriarchal Blessings Book 1, LDS Archives; copy in Irene Bates Collection. For a comprehensive treatment of the office of presiding patriarch in the LDS Church, see Irene M. Bates, "Transformation of charisma in the Mormon Church: A history of the office of Presiding Patriarch, 1833-1879," (Ph.D. Dissertation, University of California at Los Angeles, 1991). This dissertation is available from University Microfilms International (Ann Arbor, Michigan), order #9122689.

132. This will be discussed in a later section of this monograph.

priest.[133] Although Joseph Smith, Sr., was likened by this blessing to the Old Testament patriarchs, no explanation was given of his duties in the newly created office.[134] In the first year following his ordination to the office of patriarch, there is no evidence that he functioned in any other than honorary duties.

During the return of Zion's Camp to Kirtland in 1834, the subject of "patriarchal blessings" was raised by Joseph Young. His brother, Brigham, later reminisced:

> My brother, Joseph Young, and myself were in this camp. When we were on our return home my brother Joseph spoke very frequently with regard to patriarchs and patriarchal blessings, and finally said he, "When we get to Kirtland I am going to ask Brother Joseph Smith if we can have the privilege of calling our father's family together and receiving a patriarchal blessing under the hands of our father." Brother Joseph Young saw the Prophet Joseph Smith, and said he, "I do not see any inconsistency in this at all, and I think it would be a good thing." A day was appointed for the family to gather together, and Brother Joseph Smith was asked

---

133. The Irene Bates Collection contains seventy blessings given by Joseph Smith, Sr. Those that specify the authority by which Smith gave the blessings cite only the "holy priesthood." In no instance does the phrase "patriarchal priesthood" appear, thus strengthening the assertion that the 1833 use of the term "patriarchal priesthood" referred merely to the office of patriarch.

134. That the office was intended to be passed to the oldest son was indicated in a blessing that Joseph Smith, Jr., gave to his brother, Hyrum, at the same time: "He shall stand in the tracts [sic] of his father and be numbered among those who hold the right of patriarchal priesthood" (Ibid.). Blessings given by Joseph Smith, Jr., to his other brothers (Samuel, William, and Don Carlos) at the same time made no reference to "patriarchal priesthood."

to attend this meeting. He came, and while we sat chatting together on the things of the kingdom, the Prophet said, "I believe it will be necessary for Father Young to receive his patriarchal blessing and be ordained a patriarch, so that he can bless his family"; and after our little meeting was opened Brother Joseph Smith laid his hands upon Father Young and blessed him and gave him an ordination to bless his family—his own posterity. When this was done Father Young laid his hands upon the children that were there, commencing at the eldest and continuing until he had blessed all that were in the house. We were not all there, some of the brothers and sisters were absent. After that, Brother Joseph Smith said, "I think I will get my father's family together and we will have a patriarchal blessing from Father Smith." He did so. In a few days he called his father's house together and gave him the authority to bless his children, and Father Smith blessed his children. In the course of a few weeks, I think, Brother Joseph Smith received a revelation to ordain patriarchs, and he called his father's family together again, and gave his father the full ordination of patriarch for the church; and in this revelation the Lord instructed him to have a record kept, in which should be written all the blessings of the patriarch of the church, and from these circumstances were ordained a few, but only a very few, patriarchs.[135]

The first recorded blessings given by Joseph Smith, Sr., were on 9 December 1834 and only to Smith family members and their wives.[136] Beginning in 1835, he gave blessings to other church members. By the time of the

---

135. Brigham Young discourse (30 June 1873) in *Deseret News Weekly* 22, no. 25 (23 July 1873): 388.
136. Patriarchal Blessings Book 1, LDS Archives. Copies of the blessings of Hyrum and Jerusha Smith, Joseph and Emma Smith, Samuel and Mary Smith, and William Smith are in the Irene Bates Collection.

dedication of the Kirtland House of the Lord in 1836, the patriarchal blessing had become an important rite of passage for Latter Day Saints.[137]

In addressing the elders at the solemn assembly in the Kirtland House of the Lord on 30 March 1836, Joseph Smith said "that I had now completed the organization of the Church and we had passed through all the necessary ceremonies."[138] Four days later the vision of Elijah may have given him second thoughts.

Phase V: April 1836 to April 1844— Elijah and the Fulness of Priesthood

On Sunday morning, 3 April 1836, Joseph Smith and Oliver Cowdery sequestered themselves behind curtains in the House of the Lord. As they prayed they experienced a series of visions—first, of Jesus Christ, then Moses, Elias, and, finally, Elijah:

> After this vision had closed, another great and glorious vision burst upon us; for Elijah the prophet, who was taken to heaven without tasting death, stood before us, and said:
>
> Behold, the time has fully come, which was spoken of by the mouth of Malachi—testifying that he (Elijah) should be sent, before the great and dreadful day of the Lord come—
>
> To turn the hearts of the fathers to the children, and the children to the fathers, lest the whole earth be smitten with a curse—
>
> Therefore the keys of this dispensation are committed into your hands; and by this ye may know that the great

---

137. For a discussion of patriarchal blessings see Bates, chapter 5.
138. Joseph Smith diary (30 March 1836) in Scott H. Faulring, ed., *An American Prophet's Record: The Diaries and Journals of Joseph Smith* (Salt Lake City, Utah: Signature Books in association with Smith Research Associates, 1989), 155.

and dreadful day of the Lord is near, even at the doors.[139]

From an obscure figure in the early years of the Restoration, Elijah gradually emerged as the dominant figure both in priesthood and in afterlife theology. At the time of Joseph Smith's death in 1844, Elijah's importance in effecting the salvation of the world and its inhabitants was second only to Jesus Christ. To understand this extraordinary doctrinal development, it is necessary to examine the references to Elijah according to when they were written and not the time of which they speak. For example, the account of Moroni's 1823 visit to Joseph Smith, which included a promise of Elijah's return, was not written until 1838[140] and reflects the understanding and theology of the later date.

That the expectation of a return of Elijah dates to the early days of the Restoration is indicated by a revelation dated December 1830 in which the new convert, Sidney Rigdon, was told that he had unknowingly been a forerunner both of Jesus (whose return to initiate the Restoration had already occurred) and of Elijah (whose return was still anticipated).[141] However, the role of

---

139. *DC, LDS* 110: 13-16.
140. This account was written as part of Joseph Smith's history of the church. It was first published in *Times and Seasons* 3, no. 12 (15 April 1842): 753, but was not published in LDS editions of the Doctrine and Covenants until 1876; subsequent LDS editions have included it as Section 2. RLDS editions of the Doctrine and Covenants have never included this account.
141. The earliest publication of this revelation was *BC* XXXVII (1833). An earlier reference to Elijah was published in *BM, 1830*, "The Book of Nephi, the Son of Nephi, which was the Son of Helaman,"

Elijah within the Restoration was not described in this revelation, nor does any other record exist from the period between 1830 and 1835 to further clarify his role.

In preparing revelations for publication in the 1835 Doctrine and Covenants, Smith added several verses to an earlier revelation, including an important reference to Elijah. Whereas the 1830 revelation to Rigdon had stated merely that Elijah would come, the new verses said that Elijah held "the keys of the power of turning the hearts of the fathers to the children and the hearts of the children to the fathers, that the whole earth may not be smitten with a curse," repeating the essence of Malachi's prophecy.[142]

One year later, Smith and Cowdery experienced the vision of Elijah. Once again, the essence of Malachi's prophecy was unchanged: The hearts of fathers and children would be turned to each other, thus preserving the earth from a curse. Whereas the redacted revelation of 1835 spoke of keys which Elijah possessed, the vision

---

chapter XI, page 505, wherein the resurrected Christ quotes to the multitude the prophecy of Malachi. However, there is no inference in this passage of Elijah's return in the context of the Restoration.

142. *DC, 1835* XXIX: 2. In revising the text of the King James Bible, a project which Smith completed in July 1833 (see Robert J. Matthews, *"A Plainer Translation": Joseph Smith's Translation of the Bible, A History and Commentary* [Provo, Utah: Brigham Young University Press, 1975], 96), he made no changes to Malachi's prophecy of the coming of Elijah (Malachi 4: 5-6). In editing the above revelation, Smith clearly drew from the King James text, without changing its meaning. As will be seen however, subsequent references to the Malachi prophecy add new meaning to the biblical text.

of 1836 committed them to Smith and Cowdery,[143] although no explanation of such keys was given.[144]

Two years after the vision, in 1838, Smith began to dictate the history of the church. In describing the initial (1823) visit of Moroni, Smith returned again to the prophecy of Malachi. The history described Moroni quoting that prophecy with a significant change, for while earlier references to it had spoken of fathers and children turning to each other, Moroni's focused on the children, and said the earth would not merely be cursed without the turning of hearts, but "utterly wasted":

> And he [Elijah] shall plant in the hearts of the children the promises made to the fathers, and the hearts of the children shall turn to their fathers, if it were not so the whole earth would be utterly wasted at his coming.[145]

In addition, the 1838 account quoted Moroni as linking (for the first time) Elijah and priesthood: "Behold, I will reveal unto you the Priesthood by the hand of Elijah the prophet before the coming of the great and dreadful day of the Lord.[146]

In the summer of 1839 Joseph Smith gave a discourse on priesthood in which he again referred to

---

143. *DC, LDS* 110: 16.
144. The turning of hearts of fathers and children to each other is now associated by the LDS Church with the temple-based ordinance of "sealing" children to parents. However, at the time of this vision (1836) neither the word "seal" nor the concept or the formal ordinance had been mentioned.
145. Dean C. Jessee, ed. *The Personal Writings of Joseph Smith* (Salt Lake City, Utah: Deseret Book, 1984), 204. Although not making an explicit reference to deceased fathers, this account represents an incremental step toward a developing doctrine of salvation of the dead through the intervention of the living, as will subsequently be described.
146. Ibid. Several lines of evidence suggest strongly that this account, though cast in a setting of 1823, reflects the understanding of

Elijah, this time making explicit a necessary relationship between living and dead:

> The hearts of the children will have to be turned to the fathers, & the fathers to the children living or dead to prepare them for the coming of the Son of Man. If Elijah did not come the whole earth would be smitten.[147]

The following summer, Smith gave form to the relationship between living and dead when he announced that it was the privilege of the Latter Day Saints to be baptized in behalf of their deceased kin who had died without baptism.[148]

1838 and is thus anachronistic. First, as has been shown in this monograph, the term "priesthood" was not used to describe restored authority until 1832—three years after the restoration events and nine years after the initial Moroni visit. Second, all earlier accounts of the Moroni visits failed to mention either Elijah or priesthood. Third, no Restoration reference to Elijah before the 1838 account mentions or even infers a relationship between Elijah and priesthood. Fourth, the sequential redactions of Malachi 4:6, which formed the basis of a developing theology of afterlife, demonstrate a continuum; the 1838 redaction, with its inference toward salavation of the dead, fits logically only between the 1836 vision of Elijah, which lacks such inference, and an 1839 reference to Elijah (to be discussed subsequently), which for the first time explicitly links living and dead.

147. Although some writers have dated this sermon 2 July 1839, it appears more appropriate to leave the date uncertain but before 8 August 1839. For a detailed explanation of the dating of the discourse, see Andrew F. Ehat and Lyndon W. Cook, eds., *The Words of Joseph Smith: The Contemporary Accounts of the Nauvoo Discourses of the Prophet Joseph Smith* (Provo, Utah: Religious Studies Center, Brigham Young University, 1980), 22.

148. Smith made the announcement during a sermon at the funeral of Seymour Brunson on 15 August 1840. Eyewitness accounts of the sermon, written by Jane Neymon and Simon Baker, are in the "Journal History" of the LDS Church under that date.

On 5 October 1840 Smith returned to the relationship of Elijah and priesthood. In what was apparently the only discourse for which he ever prepared a text, he acknowledged that, in spite of the restoration events of 1829, 1831, and 1836, there was more to "priesthood" than had yet been revealed:

As it is generally supposed that Sacrifice was entirely done away when the great sacrif[ic]e was offered up— and that there will be no necessity for the ordinance of Sacrifice in the future, but those who assert this, are certainly not acquainted with the duties, privileges and authority of the priesthood. or with the prophets[.] The offering of Sacrifice has ever been connected and forms a part of the duties of the priesthood. It began with the pries[t]hood and will be continued untill after the coming of Christ from generation to generation—We freequently have mention made of the offering of Sacrifice by the servants of the most high in antient days prior to the law of moses, See which ordinances will be continued *when the priesthood is restored with all its authority power and blessings.* Elijah was the last prophet that held the keys of this priesthood, and who will, before the last dispensation, restore the authority and delive[r] the Keys of this priesthood in order that all the ordinances may be attended to in righteousness.

It is true the Saviour had authority and power to bestow this blessing but the Sons of Levi were too prejudi[ced]. And I will send Elijah the Prophet before the great and terrible day of the Lord &c., &c.

Why send Elijah because he holds the Keys of the Authority to administer in all the ordinances of the priesthood and without the authority is given the ordinances could not be administered in righteousness.[149]

---

149. Joseph Smith discourse (5 October 1840), emphasis added. The original manuscript, in the hand of Robert B. Thompson, is in the LDS Archives. The discourse was published in its entirety in Ehat and Cook, 38-44.

This discourse was important for two reasons. First, it stated explicitly that the concept of priesthood was fluid, that one could not point to a single date and claim that was when "the priesthood was restored." The events of 1829, 1831, and 1836 were all part of the gradual restoration of priesthood, a restoration best understood as process rather than event. Second, it went beyond the 1838 history, not only linking Elijah and priesthood, but placing Elijah at the forefront of priesthood. (Perhaps it is not surprising that on only one occasion after this discourse did Joseph Smith ever refer to the restoration events of 1829 and 1831—and that reference, which simply mentioned an unnamed angel who restored authority to baptize, was part of a larger discourse highlighting the priority of Elijah's authority.[150])

One year after the initiation of baptisms for the dead, Smith delivered a discourse on that subject that specifically linked Elijah to the restoration of the ordinance.[151] Two epistles written by Joseph Smith in September 1842 further reinforced the relationship between Elijah, priesthood, and salvation of the dead.

---

150. That occasion was a discourse in the Nauvoo Temple (10 March 1844). The accounts of the discourse, which will be analyzed later in this monograph, were published in Ehat and Cook, 327-336. The emerging importance of Elijah, coupled with the deemphasis by Smith of John the Baptist and Peter, James, and John, raises the question of why the LDS and RLDS churches today give strong emphasis to the relationship of the latter to priesthood, yet virtually ignore the priority that Smith accorded to Elijah. This question will be addressed in a later section of this monograph.

151. Joseph Smith discourse (3 October 1841); published in Ehat and Cook, 76-79.

The first, written 1 September, stated "for I am about to restore many things to the earth, saith the Lord of Hosts."[152] The second, written five days later, connected Saint Paul's reference to being "baptized for the dead" (I Corinthians 15:29) to the mission of Elijah. Quoting Malachi's prophecy of Elijah, Smith continued:

> The earth will be smitten with a curse unless there is a welding link of some kind between the fathers and the children, upon some subject or other—and behold what is that subject? It is the baptism for the dead. For we without them cannot be made perfect; neither can they without us be made perfect.... It is necessary...that a whole and complete and perfect union, and welding together of dispensations, and keys, and powers, and glories should take place.[153]

According to this epistle, not only would the earth be wasted without the mission of Elijah, but also the perfection of Smith's audience—the living—depended on their union with the dead through the ordinance of baptism.

A year later, in August 1843, Smith applied for the first time the term "sealing" to the relationship between parents and children, invoking in the process the name of Elijah:

> A measure of this sealing is to confirm upon their head in common with Elijah the doctrine of election or the

---

152. DC, LDS 127:8. This epistle was first published in Times and Seasons 3, no. 22 (15 September 1842): 919-920.

153. DC, LDS 128:18. This epistle was first published in Times and Seasons 3, no. 23 (1 October 1842): 934-936. Although the similarity between "welding" and "sealing" is obvious, the latter term had not yet been used in the context of binding one person to another (in this case, child to parent), although in 1831 it had been used in a related context wherein "sealing up to eternal life" indicated a binding of the individual to God.

covenant with Abraham—which when a Father & mother of a family have entered into[,] their children who have not transgressed are secured by the seal where with the Parents have been sealed.[154]

Two weeks later Smith preached a sermon on priesthood. Deriving his remarks from the seventh chapter of Hebrews, he stated that the author of the epistle was referring to *three* priesthoods: Melchizedek, Patriarchal, and Aaronic (or Levitical).[155] Of these, only the Aaronic and Patriarchal had yet been experienced in the church. While it sounds inconsistent to say that the highest of the three, Melchizedek, did not yet exist in the church, despite the term having been the preferred name of higher authority since 1835, it is under-

---

154. Joseph Smith discourse at the funeral of Judge Elias Higbee (13 August 1843). Accounts of this discourse by Willard Richards, Howard and Martha Coray, Franklin D. Richards, William Clayton, and Levi Richards were published in Ehat and Cook, 238-242. The passage quoted here is from the Coray account.
155. Ibid., 243-248. The account of Franklin D. Richards reported:
    There are 3 grand principles or orders of Priesthood portrayed in this chapter
    1st Levitical which was never able to administer a Blessing but only to bind heavy burdens which neither they nor their father able to bear
    2 Abrahams Patriarchal power which is the greatest yet experienced in this church
    3d That of Melchisedec who had still greater power.... (Page 245)
    James Burgess wrote:
    Hebrewes 7 cvhap. Paul is here treating of three priesthood, namely the preisthood of Aron, Abraham, and Melchizedek, Abraham's preisthood was of greater power than Levi's and Melchizedeck's was of greater power than that of Abraham. (Page 247)
    Levi Richards wrote:
    J. Smith...afterwards preached from Hebrews 7 upon the priesthood Aaronic, Patriarchal, & Melchisedec. (Page 247)

standable when viewed in the context of concurrent doctrinal developments. Having established in 1840 that the priesthood "with all its authority power and blessings" had not yet been restored, Smith was now to embark upon the ultimate step in its restoration. Only one month after this discourse, he bestowed upon members of his inner circle (men and women) the "Second Anointing," also termed the "fulness of the Priesthood."[156] Recognizing that this went well beyond anything previously restored, and wishing to place it in a separate category, he used the text of Hebrews 7 to validate the concept of three priesthoods, rather than the two which previously had been formulated. In this text, Abraham (a patriarch) paid tithes to Melchizedek and was thus portrayed as subordinate to him. Having previously associated Abraham (and the other Old Testament patriarchs) with Melchizedek Priesthood, Smith merely kept the essence of what had been called Melchizedek Priesthood, renamed it after the patriarchs, ("Patriarchal Priesthood"), and applied the former term to the new order. Because the Second Anointing had not been introduced at the time of this sermon, Smith was correct in saying that the newly renamed Patriarchal Priesthood was the greatest yet experienced in the church.[157]

---

156. For discussions of this subject, see Andrew F. Ehat, "Joseph Smith's Introduction of Temple Ordinances and the 1844 Mormon Succession Question" (M.A. Thesis, Brigham Young University, 1982); and David J. Buerger, "'The Fulness of the Priesthood': The Second Anointing in Latter-day Saint Theology and Practice," *Dialogue* 16, no. 1 (1983): 10-44.

157. Brigham Young, knowing of the forthcoming Second Anointing, had commented three weeks earlier that if any in the church had the Melchizedek Priesthood, he did not know it. "For any

In discussing the highest of the three priesthoods (now to be called Melchizedek), Smith again invoked the name of Elijah, stating: "how shall god come to the rescue of this generation. he shall send Elijah."[158]

On 21 January 1844 Joseph Smith delivered a sermon in which he summarized the mission of Elijah as he then understood it:

> What is the object of this important mission [of Elijah] or how is it to be fulfilled, The keys are to be deliverd the spirit of Elijah is to Come, The gospel to be esstablished the Saints of God gatherd Zion built up, & the Saints to Come up as Saviors on mount Zion but how are they to become Saviors on Mount Zion by building their temples erecting their Baptismal fonts & going forth & receiving all the ordinances, Baptisms, confirmations, washings anointings ordinations & sealing powers upon our heads in behalf of all our Progenitors who are dead & redeem them that they may come forth in the first resurrection & be exalted to thrones of glory with us, & herein is the chain that binds the hearts of the fathers to the children & the children to the Fathers *which fulfills the mission of Elijah.*[159]

Not only had Elijah become the paramount figure in priesthood theology, he now was seen to be primarily responsible for all salvific ordinances for the living and the dead. Three months before his own death, Smith reinforced Elijah's position at the pinnacle of priesthood and, indeed, the entire kingdom of God on the earth:

---

person to have the fulness of that priesthood he must be a king & a Priest" (Wilford Woodruff diary, 6 August 1843, in Scott G. Kenney, ed., *Wilford Woodruff's Journal* 2 [Salt Lake City, Utah: Signature Books, 1983], 271).

158. Ehat and Cook, 244.

159. Joseph Smith discourse (21 January 1844), emphasis added, in Wilford Woodruff diary (21 January 1844); also in Ehat and Cook, 318.

The spirit power & calling of Elijah is that ye have power to hold the keys of the revelations, ordinances, oracles, powers & endowments of the fulness of the Melchizedek Priesthood & of the Kingdom of God on the Earth & to receive, obtain & perform all the ordinances belonging to the Kingdom of God even unto the sealing of the hearts of the fathers unto the children & the hearts of the children unto the fathers even those who are in heaven....

This is the spirit of Elijah that we redeem our dead & connect ourselves with our fathers which are in heaven & seal up our dead to come forth in the first resurrection & here we want the power of Elijah to seal those who dwell on earth to those who dwell in heaven. This is the power of Elijah & the keys of the Kingdom of Jehovah.[160]

In the same discourse Smith reverted to a bipartite model of priesthood, after only six months of the tripartite model. Patriarchal Priesthood was now folded into Melchizedek Priesthood, which continued to include the "fulness of the Priesthood," or Second Anointing.[161]

Smith's final reference to Elijah came in the famous King Follett Sermon on 7 April 1844 when he stated "the greatest responsibility in this world is to seek after our dead," and equated that responsibility with the mission of Elijah.[162]

---

160. Joseph Smith discourse (10 March 1844), in Wilford Woodruff diary (10 March 1844). The account of Woodruff, plus those of James Burgess, Franklin D. Richards, Willard Richards, Thomas Bullock, and John Solomon Fullmer were published in Ehat and Cook, 327-336.

161. The Lesser Priesthood had undergone little change since 1835, although a variety of synonyms—Aaronic, Levitical, Lesser, and Priesthood of Elias—had been used at various times. It was not changed by Smith's reversion to the bipartite model.

162. Joseph Smith discourse (7 April 1844), in William Clayton account. This and other accounts of the discourse were published in Ehat and Cook, 340-362.

Summary

In reviewing the development of Latter Day Saint priesthood during Joseph Smith's ministry, one might be reminded of the work of Harvard biologist Stephen Jay Gould, who described biological evolution as "punctuated equilibrium"—that is, a gradual process of development, accented at irregular intervals by major changes over brief periods of time. In the case of priesthood, the "punctuation marks" are readily identifiable and, with the single exception of the restoration of the High Priesthood, involved angelic intervention:

- **1823-1827:** The visits of Moroni, guardian of the gold plates, through whose ministry to Joseph Smith came implicit authority to begin a religious movement.
- **1829:** The visits of John the Baptist, who restored authority to baptize, and of Peter, James, and John, who restored the apostleship.
- **1831:** The "endowment" of power from on high, through ordination to the High Priesthood. (Although this did not involve specific angelic intervention, it was a pentecostal experience rivaling that of the ancient Pentecost.)
- **1836:** The vision of Elijah.

Between the punctuation marks came periods of incremental change, as Joseph Smith gradually came to understand the implications of his visionary experiences, and changed policy and doctrine to reflect his own understanding. Nevertheless, these "quiet periods" were of enormous significance, seen most clearly in the case of the theology surrounding Elijah. Whereas the vision of Elijah was of unquestionable significance, he was but one of four figures appearing to Smith and

Cowdery. It was not the vision alone but the added process of reflection, prayer, and gradual enlightenment over the following eight years that moved Elijah from an obscure figure to one of virtually unparalleled importance.

In summary, the development of the notion of priesthood is evident in the contemporary accounts of the early years of the Restoration. Five relatively distinct phases have been identified:

I. Before April 1829 (a period of "implicit authority"): In the earliest years no explicit notion of authority was mentioned in any records relating to the Restoration. Joseph Smith acted in his unique position by virtue of his relationship with Moroni, rather than formal ordination.

II. Between April 1829 and October 1830 (a period of "angelic authority"): The dictation of passages from the Book of Mormon dealing with baptism was followed by an April 1829 angelic bestowal on Joseph Smith and Oliver Cowdery of authority to baptize each other. Dictation several weeks later of passages referring to twelve disciples or elders, with authority to confer the Holy Ghost and ordain priests and teachers (the latter offices identified within the Book of Mormon as having the authority to baptize), again was followed in early June 1829 by angelic bestowal on Smith and Cowdery of authority to ordain other officers and to confer the Holy Ghost. The term "priesthood" was not used to refer to either level of authority. Rather, men acted by virtue of the office to which they had been ordained.

"Elder" and "disciple," as described in the Book of Mormon, were interchangeable terms and implied authority equal to that of the twelve apostles of Jerusalem. By the latter part of 1829, the term "apostle" was used within the Restoration, rather than "disciple." It was later explained that "elder" was an administrative title used during ministrations, while "apostle" seems to have referred to the role of the same men as witnesses of Jesus Christ. By the end of 1830 (apparently shortly before or in conjunction with the ordination of twelve men to these offices), the titles of apostle and elder were separated, with new elders no longer carrying the second title.

III. Between December 1830 and November 1831 (introduction of the High Priesthood): In December 1830 Sidney Rigdon, troubled by what he perceived to be a lack of tangible power in the missionaries who had converted him, traveled to New York and quickly became an aide to Joseph Smith. The following month Smith announced a revelation promising that the elders soon would be "endowed with power from on high" in preparation for their forthcoming missions. Two February revelations suggested this endowment would come in a conference in Kirtland. Shortly thereafter, as Smith revised the book of Genesis, he added several verses describing an ancient order to which Melchizedek had been ordained as a high priest, which possessed immense this-worldly powers. A revelation in May suggested that the endowment would come through ordination to this order. The anticipated endowment of "power from on high," which was accompanied by a pentecostal outpouring of miracles, came at a conference in June 1831 through ordination to a new order called both the Order of Melchizedek and the High Priesthood. This did not yet refer to the office of high priest which, though appearing in the Book of Mormon, was not yet applied to individuals in the Restoration.

The following October, Smith carried Restoration theology beyond the grave by announcing that the new High Priesthood included authority to seal the Saints "unto eternal life." A revelation the following month established the office of high priest, which then became synonymous with High Priesthood.

IV. Between November 1831 and March 1836 (a period of "organizational development"): During these important years a number of parallel yet interrelated developments took place. Church government was centralized, with Joseph Smith being designated "President of the High Priesthood." Four governing bodies—high councils, bishoprics, the Quorum of the Twelve Apostles, and the First Quorum of the Seventy— were formed to assist in governing the church, but Smith's primacy over all these bodies was explicit.

The offices of elder, priest, teacher, and deacon were organized into formal groups, each with a president chosen from among its members and given responsibility for their spiritual welfare.

Amidst these organizational developments, a new understanding of priesthood emerged. Through mid-1832 the term was used exclusively in conjunction with High Priesthood, which initially referred to an order of elders and then to the office of high priest. In September of that year, a revelation extended usage of the term, referring to the authority to baptize as "lesser priesthood" and to the higher authority as "holy priesthood." Additionally, the revelation created a hierarchy of offices, with bishops and elders being appendages to high priests, while teachers and deacons were appendages to priests. Two and a half years later the final step was taken, which transformed the term "priesthood" to its modern, generic usage. In a revelation in March 1835, priests, teachers, and deacons were all described as offices *within* the Aaronic Priesthood, while elders and high priests were *within* the Melchizedek Priesthood.

Two other organizational developments during this time related to the spiritual status of church members. Elders were told that there was a continuing need for them to receive an endowment of "power from on high" to qualify them for missionary labors. The concepts of "endowment" and "sacred space" came together with the construction of the Kirtland House of the Lord, and anticipation of a pentecostal endowment of the elders (which occurred in March 1836) became the primary driving force leading to the completion of the building. Simultaneous with the development of "endowment theology" was the initiation of patriarchal blessings, in which Joseph Smith, Sr., conferred on individual church members blessings of comfort, direction, and revelation.

V. April 1836 to April 1844 (Elijah and the "fulness of priesthood"): Shortly after the 1835 revelation transforming "priesthood" into its new generic role, Joseph Smith first identified the angels who years before had bestowed on him the authority to baptize and ordain. Respectively, they were John the Baptist and Peter, James, and John. Just a year later, however, their roles in the Restoration began to be eclipsed by the Old Testament prophet, Elijah, a figure previously alluded to by Smith only cryptically. Over a period of eight years, beginning in 1836, it gradually became apparent that through Elijah's instrumentality all salvific ordinances, both for the living and the dead, were made both possible and essential. By the time of Smith's death, Elijah's position in Restoration theology was second only to that of Jesus Christ. Thus, it is curious that both of the major Latter Day Saint churches today have deemphasized Elijah's role in priesthood theology. While one cannot be certain, it appears that this phenomenon developed because of the defection, and subsequent return to the church of Oliver Cowdery.

Cowdery had participated with Smith in each of the angelic ministrations associated with priesthood (named as John the Baptist and Peter, James, and John in 1829; and Elijah in 1836). However, at the time of Cowdery's dissociation and subsequent excommunication from the church in 1838, Joseph Smith had not even begun to make the association between Elijah, priesthood, and salvation theology. During the entire period of development of Elijah theology (1838-1844), Cowdery was out of the church and physically removed from the Saints; hence, he would have been unaware of the developing theology (most of which was not published during Smith's life), and would have accorded Elijah no greater status than the other participants in the 1836 visions. At the time Cowdery left, there were two priesthoods only—Aaronic and Melchizedek—both of which had become associated with the events of 1829, and neither of which was associated (at that time) with Elijah.

Shortly after Smith's death, Cowdery began to show renewed interest in the church, eventually rejoining it in 1848. In 1846, writing to Phineas Young, he spoke only of the events of 1829:

> I have been sensitive on this subject, I admit; but I ought to be so—you would be, under the circumstances, had you stood in the presence of John, with our departed Joseph, to receive the Lesser Priesthood—and in the presence of Peter, to receive the Greater, and look down

through time, and witness the effects these two must produce.[163]

Similarly, when he reentered the church in 1848, he recounted the restoration events of 1829 but was silent concerning Elijah.[164] Because Cowdery was the only living witness to the events he described, it is likely that his audience, both immediate and extended, focused on what he described (the events of 1829), not on what he did *not* describe (the 1836 vision of Elijah and the subsequent doctrinal developments). Such a sequence of events, while not certain, would explain the otherwise baffling silence of both churches on a matter so overwhelmingly important to Joseph Smith.[165]

The study of early Latter Day Saint priesthood affords an opportunity of understanding a related topic, the doctrine of revelation. Both Latter Day Saint churches rest on a foundation of continuing revelation, yet it is likely that few within either church understand it. Indeed, although it is the principle underlying all other

---

163. Oliver Cowdery to Phineas Young (23 March 1846), Ms 3408 fd 3, LDS Archives. This letter was quoted in an LDS General Conference address by Alonzo A. Hinckley on 8 April 1934 and published in *Conference Reports* (April 1934): 129.

164. Reuben Miller journal (21 October 1848), Ms 1392, LDS Archives.

165. The role of Elijah in Latter Day Saint theology has yet to be explored in detail. The importance of the subject to Joseph Smith suggests the value of a future study of the theology of Elijah during the ministry of Joseph Smith and subsequently within the LDS and RLDS traditions. An alternative explanation for the fading of Elijah's prominence in Latter Day Saint theology following Smith's death was that the church membership, in general, simply did not understand Elijah theology in the same light as Smith. Because Smith was the sole exponent of the theology, it is possible that his death, and the abrupt halt it brought to the developing theology, was sufficient of itself to effect the subsequent silence on the subject.

doctrines, it defies direct examination and is best understood by examining other core doctrines, such as priesthood. In contrast to the conception of many (perhaps most) Latter Day Saints that revelation is "propositional"[166]—that is, God dispenses revelation as prepackaged entities, the role of the prophet merely being to unwrap the package—the historical record indicates that revelation may best be described as "process punctuated by event" and that the human is as crucial as the divine in defining the process.

---

166. For a discussion of "propositional revelation" within the Latter Day Saint traditions, see Richard P. Howard, "Latter Day Saint Scripture and the Doctrine of Propositional Revelation," *Courage: A Journal of History, Thought and Action* 1, no. 4 (1971): 209-225.

Response

Gregory A. Prince presented an abbreviated version of this monograph at the annual meeting of the Mormon History Association in St. George, Utah, on May 15, 1992. The following response to that paper, given at the meeting by Paul M. Edwards, Temple School Center director of the Reorganized Church of Jesus Christ of Latter Day Saints, is presented here with permission of its author.

It is always a pleasure to comment on a well-constructed, carefully researched, and nicely written paper; especially one that was sent in its entirety at least a month before the delivery date. Being a scientist at heart, Dr. Prince has not yet learned the methods of procrastination used by the old-time historians, thus he actually presented the same paper he made available for me to read and to comment upon.

Dr. Prince's research is excellent. This paper, a part of a larger and more complex presentation, is the result of years of work in which he has amassed almost every conceivable bit of information available. His interpretations, calm and responsible, are equally good examples of well-focused and defined research.

Thus, since he robbed me of the meat of 90 percent of most replies, I will move beyond the usual *ad homenie* attacks and direct my attention to comments upon the work itself—dangerous at best for there are several points that I might make, some for clarification, some for reasoned disagreement, and at least one comment because this is perhaps the only chance I will have to make the observation.

I am a little unclear about the difference expressed in his paper between implicit and explicit authority. Primarily authority lies with the prophetic experience which men and women believe—and with the charismatic leader who made it believable. It was only when necessary to convince other persons of the power of disagreement, the need to supply weight to otherwise questionable positions, that authority became necessary. The parallel growth of the offices of the priesthood and the organization growth of the movement would seem to be as valid an explanation as the assumption of pyramid revelation.

My father spent most of my young life as a member of the First Presidency of the Reorganization. My mother taught English literature at the University of Kansas City. When they would disagree over some point of literature and my father raised his presidential voice, my mother would respond, "Frank, I know you have authority. But I *am* an authority." There is a difference. What is that difference in the Mormon priesthood?

The difficult question, of course, lies in the authority of the prophet who was *necessarily* to have and to be an authority at the same time. He needed a system where those who were responsible only *had* authority, thus weakening the power of those who *were* authorities.

I am also aware of some confusion over Dr. Prince's strong emphasis on the particular meaning and precise selection of words. It seems to me that the careful and sophisticated selection of terms takes on an accelerated meaning after the fact. When speaking about a spiritual experience, a prophet may not worry too much whether he calls the visiting messenger an angel or an elder while, after the fact, we may well make too much of whatever term he used. I am not sure just how many theological affirmations can be drawn from the chronology of the use of words when the words were, at the time, without clear definition, and—at the time of use—carried no theological baggage.

By the same token, I think his case would be stronger had he sought some historical connectedness. Remembering that while every historical fact opens itself to eternity, every eternal fact also occurs in a moment of history. There is only local history, for events—no matter how earthshaking—occur in a time and a place. It may well sound paradoxical and thus unwarranted, but consider that in history synthesis occurs in the act of the analysis itself and thus is always seen reflected by the landscape against which it is identified. That is, it occurs in a time and a place both of which are essential to the understanding of the acceptance—hence the meaning—of the event. "Men's lives," Bayard Taylor tells us, "are chains of chance and history their sun."

In this case, I suppose, the question is: What does the corporate life do to mystical experience? On the positive side, corporate life gives such experience an environment, an environment in which it can happen and can be dealt with. Yet we would be wise to remember Zenas Gurley, Jr., of the Reorganization who challenged prophetic power and pushed for more democratic control because he believed that Joseph Smith, Jr., had perverted the Christian nature of the movement by making himself "not the prophet he was called to be, but 'an essential part of the gospel'" (Clare D. Vlahos, "The Challenge to Centralized Power: Zenas H. Gurley, Jr., and the Prophetic Office," *Courage* 1, no. 3 [1971]: 143).

As both the dispenser and receiver of the authority of the gospel, it is inconceivable to imagine that Joseph himself was not a major source of the meaning and, in turn, the recipient of considerable environmental saturation. How this effect would be felt, and how it affects the nature of the mystical experience, will be hard to define but dangerous to ignore.

A second comment arises from my own logical training, not to be confused, you understand, with logical thinking. It calls me to wonder, however, about the two or three times Dr. Prince falls into the fallacy of unification. I refer, as an example, to a comment he makes concerning the office/orders of apostle and elder, "stating that 'An apostle is an elder.'" Dr. Prince will note, if he thinks about it, that inclusion is not the same as identity, that for one to be included in the other does not mean that they are the same.

My point is to suggest that reductionism—which Prince discovers—is not a particularly good method for identifying theological understanding.

Another explanation—and one found in some aspects of the RLDS community—is that each priesthood office includes the previous; that is, an elder encompasses the role of deacon, teacher, priest, etc.

It is equally true that to define the limits of a case is not to define the limits of a class. For example, it needs to be noted that when one organizes a group identified as the Quorum of Twelve Apostles, that this does not, in itself, mean there are only twelve apostles. It may well mean that some twelve of them are identified as a quorum. There may well be seventy apostles (just to pick a number), and the rest are simply not in quorums.

As an aside, if Dr. Prince is going to make such a case for the differences between an office and an order, he might well provide us with some definition of the difference.

A third comment arises from Dr. Prince's use of the term "received" for his presentation of revelation materials, assuming, I suppose, that anything Joseph spoke of as being spiritual was thus "received." I would not be true to myself if I did not question the meaning of revelation in this matter. For, I think, I am reading Prince as identifying revelation as any theological issue which emerges in a great outpouring of concern.

Thus I would ask first, (a) What is the nature of revelation that is provided in such a spotty and internally contradictory manner? Do the questions of coherence, correspondence, consistency, contingency, and consequential relations apply? Can one expect prophets to speak rationally? And if they do not, what can be gained by a rational analysis of their work?

And second, (b) I am forced to wonder again—not so much in response to Dr. Prince's comments but in response to my concerns—what is the place of, and the line between, sacred concept (expression) and sacred space? Especially, I would add, for a movement that has been busting its public relations buttons to assure the world that we are indeed attached to a transcendental divinity. It may be enough at this point to simply say that Dr. Prince's paper—like so much of what we discover about our movement—raises some very significant questions about the nature of revelation.

I wish also to simply admit to some confusion in my mind about the explanation given for the loss of—or perhaps it is only the misplacement of—the concept of Patriarchal Priesthood. Simply to suggest that Cowdery was out of favor during the discussions, and thus was not able to serve as a bridge of transmittal between generations, is to place too much on Cowdery. And it suggests a simplicity to the organization and structure of the movement that Dr. Prince's own paper denies. There has to be a better (or maybe I simply want a different) explanation.

I am constantly amazed at how I can be constantly amazed at the complexity of the attempts both to figure out, and assign meaning to, our uncovered roots. If all this happened as Prince suggests, and I can but believe that it did, and if the presentation of the priesthood and authority is reflective of the movement's organizational beginnings, then I am amazed once again. The organization and creation of the movement is very much an unfolding event, much like children who are busy making up rules for a new game even as they play it. It is a game where an older, more arrogant child dominates the game by insisting on rules designed to place him or her in a better and better position to change the rules.

I hope it comes as no insult to my dear friend Greg Prince, nor to any of you whom I would hate to embarrass, but you do know that if we were not already believers, if we were not accustomed to hearing such wonderful stories and giving them meaning, were we not so attached to the conclusion that we assume the beginning, that we would be astounded at such a story. Astounded that anyone would expect us to respond to such a development in any other manner than to say that the church, much like the British government these several centuries, survived by generous application of the management style known as "muddling through."

Contemporary priesthood authority lies in the authority given persons on the basis of the power of priesthood. It is a tautology. And, historically, I must wonder how much priesthood authority is the result of the enfolding of divine instruction and how much is the acceptable adaptation of such power by persons and by groups who, thus identified, are able to make their authority felt. The big kids, having discovered the power of class identity, have complicated the classes to make sure they support the big kids in their identification of new rules.

If there is any value in my suspicions, then we would be wise to remember Pope's most familiar lines: "Know then thyself! Presume not God to scan! The proper study of mankind is man." I do not agree with Pope, that the problems of theology and speculative metaphysics are too vast and complicated for the human mind to consider. Rather, people should not be seen too simply as a tool for a complicated God. People are such vast and complicated beasts themselves that they should, perhaps, be studied first. A good sociological evaluation of the emergence of priesthood is certainly in order here.

Perhaps I protest too much. But I find myself in the same state of mind as the ancient historian who remarked of Rome that she could no longer endure either her vices or their remedies. Perhaps the historian did not define her own epoch as much as our Mormon studies. I wonder what is more difficult to understand: the process or the reason that we find God in it.

This leads me to make a comment which I have unashamedly attached to these remarks for personal reasons. It has to do with a gentle shifting of the priesthood fault line, with the potential earthquake that haunts some thinking persons. I speak here of the growing questions about the nature of priesthood, the necessity of such office or ordination, the value of the "office of member" as the RLDS define it, the hierarchial disfavor reflected in priesthood, and finally—though it is not very nice to say about your own people and, I assure you, the very opposite of my own point of view—the as-yet-unsettled belief that if women can be priesthood members then priesthood can't be all that it was cracked up to be.

I have no statistics yet—we don't keep statistics on things these days—but it is my observation that as more and more women get involved in priesthood responsibility more and more men withdraw. Not, I assure you, from disagreement as much as from burnout, from relief that another can, at last, help with the burden. But again, we need someone with more sociological training than I have.

Some of this burnout, however, reflects the self-identification aspects of priesthood—that aspect which allows a man whose job and economic situation give him no standing, to have standing. These trappings of power are lessening, the expectations of authority diminishing. These changes, and the widening of the selection base, all work to make the role of the priesthood member less elite, thus less significant in self-identification.

Perhaps this phenomenon is not at stake in the LDS movement. But, at least to some degree, I tend to think it is. I don't know what I want anyone to do about it; I am not even sure I am in disagreement with what I think is happening, but it is yet another shifting sand upon which so many have built their metaphysical homes.

Having said all this, let me close with an affirmation of the excellent work Dr. Prince has done, to express my appreciation, even my wonder, at the extent of his research, to support much of his analysis, and to support him by encouraging you to make yourself aware of his larger and more elaborate perspective when it is available. It is, and will be, a major, if not a definitive, accomplishment.

Paul M. Edwards

Bibliography

A Book of Commandments, for the Government of the Church of Christ, Organized According to Law, on the 6th of April, 1830. Independence, Missouri: W. W. Phelps & Co., 1833.

Arrington, Leonard J. "Oliver Cowdery's Kirtland, Ohio, 'Sketch Book,'" *Brigham Young University Studies* 12, no. 4 (1972).

The Book of Mormon: An Account Written by the Hand of Mormon, Upon Plates Taken from the Plates of Nephi. Palmyra, New York: E. B. Grandin, 1830.

Buerger, David J. "'The Fulness of the Priesthood': The Second Anointing in Latter-day Saint Theology and Practice," *Dialogue* 16, no. 1 (1983).

Cannon, Donald Q. "Licensing in the Early Church," *Brigham Young University Studies* 22, no. 1 (Winter 1982).

Cannon, Donald Q., and Lyndon W. Cook, eds. *Far West Record: Minutes of the Church of Jesus Christ of Latter-day Saints, 1830-1844.* Salt Lake City, Utah: Deseret Books, 1983.

Cook, Lyndon W. *The Revelations of the Prophet Joseph Smith.* Provo, Utah: Seventy's Mission Bookstore, 1981.

Corrill, John. *Brief History of the Church of Christ of Latter Day Saints (commonly called Mormons); Including an Account of their Doctrine and Discipline; With the Reasons of the Author for Leaving the Church.* St. Louis: printed for the author, 1839.

Cowdery, Oliver. "The Articles of the Church of Christ" (1829). Original in Archives Division, Church Historical Department, The Church of Jesus Christ of Latter-day Saints, Salt Lake City, Utah.

Doctrine and Covenants of The Church of the Latter Day Saints: Carefully Selected from the Revelations of God. Kirtland, Ohio: F. G. Williams & Co., 1835.

Doxey, Roy W. *The Doctrine and Covenants Speaks.* Salt Lake City, Utah: Deseret Books, 1970.

Ehat, Andrew F., and Lyndon W. Cook, eds. *The Words of Joseph Smith: The Contemporary Accounts of the Nauvoo Discourses of the Prophet Joseph Smith.* Provo, Utah: Religious Studies Center, Brigham Young University, 1980.

Edwards, F. Henry. *A Commentary on the Doctrine and Covenants.* Independence, Missouri: Herald Publishing House, 1967.

Faulring, Scott H., ed. *An American Prophet's Record: The Diaries and Journals of Joseph Smith.* Salt Lake City, Utah: Signature Books in association with Smith Research Associates, 1989.

General Handbook of Instructions. Salt Lake City, Utah: Corporation of the President of The Church of Jesus Christ of Latter-day Saints, 1989.

Hartley, William G. *They Are My Friends: A History of the Joseph Knight Family, 1825-1850.* Provo, Utah: Grandin Books, 1986.

Howard, Richard P. "Latter Day Saint Scripture and the Doctrine of Propositional Revelation," *Courage: A Journal of History, Thought and Action* 1, no. 4 (1971): 209-225.

Howe, E. D. *Mormonism Unvailed, or, A Faithful Account of that Singular Imposition and Delusion, From its Rise to the Present Time.* Painesville, Ohio: 1834 (reprinted in 1977 by AMS Press of New York as part of its series, "Communal Societies in America").

Jessee, Dean C. *The Personal Writings of Joseph Smith.* Salt Lake City, Utah: Deseret Books, 1984.

Joseph Smith's Kirtland Revelation Book. Salt Lake City, Utah: Modern Microfilm, 1979.

Joseph Smith's "New Translation" of the Bible. Independence, Missouri: Herald Publishing House, 1970.

Kenney, Scott G., ed. *Wilford Woodruff's Journal.* Salt Lake City, Utah: Signature Books, 1983.

Marks, Mariella, ed. *Memoirs of the Life of David Marks, Minister of the Gospel.* Dove, New Hampshire: Free-Will Baptist Printing Establishment, 1846 (first edition: 1831).

Matthew, Robert J. *"A Plainer Translation": Joseph Smith's Translation of the Bible, A History and Commentary.* Provo, Utah: Brigham Young University Press, 1975.

Pratt, Parley P. *Autobiography of Parley Parker Pratt.* Salt Lake City, Utah: Deseret Books, 1976.

"Questions asked of David Whitmer at his home in Richmond Ray County Mo. Jan 14-1835, relating to Book of Mormon, and the history of the Church of Jesus Christ of LDS by Elder Z. H. Gurley," Ms d 4681, LDS Archives, Salt Lake City, Utah. Original in Library-Archives, Reorganized Church of Jesus Christ of Latter Day Saints, Independence, Missouri.

Quinn, D. Michael. "The Evolution of the Presiding Quorums of the LDS Church," *Journal of Mormon History* 1 (1974).

Roberts, B. H. *History of the Church of Jesus Christ of Latter-day Saints*, Vols. 1-6. Salt Lake City, Utah: Deseret Books, 1896-1912.

Smith, Hyrum, and Janne M. Sjodahl. *The Doctrine and Covenants, Containing Revelations Given to Joseph Smith, Jr., The Prophet, With an Introduction and Historical and Exegetical Notes.* Salt Lake City, Utah: Deseret Books, 1960.

Smith, Joseph. "History of Joseph Smith," *Times and Seasons* 5, no. 3 (1 February 1844).

Smith, Joseph Fielding. *Church History and Modern Revelation, Being a Course of Study for the Melchizedek Priesthood Quorums for the Year 1947.* Salt Lake City, Utah: The Council of the Twelve Apostles, Deseret News Press, 1946.

Sperry, Sidney B. *Doctrine and Covenants Compendium.* Salt Lake City, Utah: Bookcraft, 1960.

The History of the Reorganized Church of Jesus Christ of Latter Day Saints, Vols. 1-8. Independence, Missouri: Herald Publishing House, 1952-1976.

Watson, Elden J., ed. *The Orson Pratt Journals.* Salt Lake City, Utah: Elden J. Watson, 1975.

Whitmer, David. *An Address to All Believers in Christ.* Richmond, Missouri: n.p., 1887.

Young, Joseph, Sr. *History of the Organization of the Seventies.* Salt Lake City, Utah: Deseret News Steam Printing Establishment, 1878.

Theses and Dissertations

Bates, Irene M. "Transformation of charisma in the Mormon Church: A history of the office of Presiding Patriarch, 1833-1879." Ph.D. Dissertation, University of California at Los Angeles, 1991.

Ehat, Andrew F. "Joseph Smith's Introduction of Temple Ordinances and the 1844 Mormon Succession Question." M.A. Thesis, Brigham Young University, 1982.

Woodford, Robert J. "The Historical Development of the Doctrine and Covenants." Ph.D. Dissertation, Brigham Young University, 1974.